THE EMAIL CEMETERY

THE EMAIL CEMETERY

WHERE BAD SALES EMAILS GO TO DIE... AND HOW TO RESUSCITATE YOURS

CHARLENE DECESARE

ISBN 978-1-950710-16-4 (Amazon Print)
ISBN 978-1-950710-17-1 (IngramSpark) PAPERBACK
ISBN 978-1-950710-18-8 (Smashwords)

For bulk purchase and for booking, contact:

CHARLENE DECESARE
CHARLENE@CHARLENEIGNITES.COM

Dedication

To Rob, who has always believed in me unconditionally, even (especially) when everyone else thought I was off my rocker.

To Makayla and Steven, who have proven that not all kids turn into monsters when they're teenagers.

To my dad, my hero, who taught me that there's a difference between hard work and struggle.

Table of Contents

In Memoriam

DEARLY BELOVED, we are gathered here today to bear witness and learn from the unfortunates who have been writing some very bad sales emails.

These poor souls are individual business owners and entrepreneurs who are struggling to pay their bills, as well as employed salespeople who are definitely not hitting their sales quotas. Along with sending these tragic emails, many of the afflicted have been heard saying things like, "I don't like to bother people" and "I don't understand why my prospects are ghosting me."

Within these pages are examples of what not to do in your sales communications, and what to do instead. My advice is based on a combination of science, education, and experience. Having worked in various sales roles since my first real job more than 35 years ago, *I seen* some things. Although I spent several years in retail, senior living, and direct consumer sales, the most notable years of my career were in business-to-business solutions at companies such as Gartner and Bright Horizons, followed by starting my own sales advisory firm. There aren't too many sales scenarios that haven't crossed my path. I've been there as an individual contributor with a big-ass quota, as a sales leader trying to keep my team motivated, and as an outsourced sales guide to a wide variety of organizations. As an entrepreneur, I've had to be a good steward of my own teachings in order to build a successful company for myself, my family, and my clients. There was also that time when my husband and I thought it would be a good idea to buy a beach bar in St. Croix.

The first piece of truly useful advice I ever received was around age three. According to my parents, I was sitting with my wooden Pound-A-Peg bench toy when I uttered the longest set of consecutive words of my life. Red-faced and frustrated, my first soliloquy was mostly expletives.

My stepmother tried not to choke on her coffee as I attempted to impel an orange peg into a similar-sized hole with a small mallet. Despite my verbal encouragement, it would not submit to my will. My dad came over to me and put one hand on mine. He said calmly, "If you're forcing it, you're doing it wrong." He had me take a breath, look at the hole more carefully, line up the peg, institute a couple of calm whacks, and *voila!* Easy peasy. Less struggle, better results.

Over the years, my dad reminded me of his words of wisdom in regards to everything from opening locks to marriage. It is also true in business, and especially in sales.

If you're forcing it, you're doing it wrong.

My goal with this book isn't just for you to see the most common sales email mistakes so you can improve your own. It's to help make sales feel fun and easy. Right now that might seem like a big leap, particularly if you're someone who would rather walk barefoot through a room full of LEGO bricks than make a cold call.

The reason sales often feels not fun or difficult is because you feel forced to do something that doesn't come naturally. Too often, traditional sales training makes this worse, not better. In all my years of selling, never did I suck more than when someone gave me a script. Worse was when a leader or trainer was listening to me recite memorized lines to a complete stranger, ready to critique every nuance as soon as I hung up the phone. One former boss actually came into my office while I was doing my first live sales call and wrote on my presentation, "TOO JOLLY! BE MORE SERIOUS!"

Naturally, I closed that deal. There's a slight possibility that smite was involved. (I ain't sayin', I just sayin'.) As it turns out, jolly is one of my specialties. My clients like jolly. More importantly, it's who I am. Being *me* is my main differentiator, just as being you is yours. I mean, have you met you?! You're awesome!

The best way to convey the full essence of *you* is during a live conversation, either in person or by phone. Video chat also works. Yet, the vast majority of business builders rely far more heavily on email. They will make excuses like, "Nobody picks up the phone anymore." Some salespeople go so far as to fudge their call numbers and enter fake "left message to call" notes into their CRM. Shocking, I know.

Many people simply feel more comfortable over email than by phone, particularly very early in the relationship. Email is patient. It waits for you to carefully craft your message, re-read, edit, step away, and edit more. Email is kind. It doesn't tie your tongue or your stomach up in knots. Email puts you in control. You can talk about your stuff and ask your questions without another human interrupting you or throwing you any curveballs.

Unfortunately, that sense of false confidence and need for control turns you into a less effective version of yourself. Forcing what you think you "should" do over email, causes you to make fundamental mistakes. You exert way too much effort for lackluster response. You end up suffering the email equivalent of Dialing for Dollars. If you make enough of these mistakes, it will sabotage your ability to make money and reach your goals. Worse, it feels gross. Nobody wants to be that guy (or gal).

The bottom line is that if you're going to send emails, it's worth being thoughtful about it. Killing an opportunity with ineffective, self-sabotaging, or icky outreach is also killing your ability to make a living, build a dream, and maybe even change the world.

The most common mistakes have been encapsulated into eight distinct sales personas addressed by chapter in this book. You may identify very closely with one or more of these personas. More likely, you'll see little familiar habits here and there. You'll read a few things in this book and think, "*Ooooo,* I totally do that!" Those are your symptoms. In some cases, fixing the symptoms will lead to vast improvement. More commonly, the symptoms are a sign of a more pervasive and serious problem.

While this book would seem to be laser-focused on sales messaging alone, the truth is that the message will always betray both the mindset and the method. For example, email communication can provide incredible insight into the head trash of an individual sales rep, as well as some dysfunction within the larger organization. You'll see a variety of specific examples of this through the lens of the eight personas. Emails are a stunning diagnostic tool.

Most of the emails that inspired the chapters of this book came straight out of my Future Clients folder in Outlook. Names and companies have been changed, as have any other details that may be identifying or proprietary. I've exercised a tiny bit of creative license here and there to make key characteristics more obvious. Also, while the subject lines have been included for most of the emails I've used here, my primary focus is on the main body text. As general advice regarding both subject lines and body text, it's worth getting cozy with CAN-SPAM Act rules and/or any other regulations for the places where you do business. You don't want your otherwise lively email to get buried in a compliance nightmare. That's a bad day.

While the emails have come to these pages to die, the people who wrote them live on. Don't kill the messenger, and all that. Most of these people had good intentions. Still, my expert guess is that all of them are (still) struggling to reach their sales quota. Even though the women of my family have a long history of psychic abilities, I don't need a crystal ball to predict sales struggle or success. Just send me an email.

A lot of people hate getting sales emails. I love it, and have been saving them for years. Often, I reply to ask if the sender would be open to some handy feedback. It's like asking someone if they'd like feedback on the beauty of their newborn baby. The less confident they are that the feedback will be positive, the more likely they are to tell me to buzz off. Ah well, it's a fun way to get off someone's contact list.

Correcting your own email habits may take practice. The more closely connected the mistake is to your current mindset, the harder it may be to change and/or the more uncomfortable it may feel. Like most things in life, it's about awareness, choices, and understanding potential consequences. There are a lot of things — eating donuts by the dozen, drinking a lot of bad whiskey, and watching too many episodes of Baywatch, for example — that may not kill you instantly, but probably will end up causing you a lot of unnecessary pain in the long run.

Pick your battles, then tackle a few things at a time. Focus on small things done, over great things planned.

1

RIP — The Egomaniac

Cause of Death: Putting the focus on the wrong person

Primary Symptoms of The Egomaniac:

- Overuse of ego words such as I, We, Me, My, Our
- Condescending words or tone
- Testimonial abuse
- Using references who bear no resemblance to the prospect
- Anything that sounds like, "Well enough about me, let's talk more about me."

Egomaniac Email Example 1

Hi Charlene,

I've been meaning to reach out and introduce myself. I don't normally reach out personally, but I came across your LinkedIn profile and think it might make sense for us to do business together.

As CEO of Gatsby Strategies, I help business owners take their personal skills to the next level in multiple areas of strategies and processes. This has made it possible for thousands of business owners I've worked with to achieve the attached list of benefits. That's why people like *<redacted>* and *<redacted>* have trusted me.

My reason for reaching out today is to see if you would be interested in learning more about what I do and how I impact organizations like yours.

Would you be available to chat this or next week?

If it helps, here's a bit more about me to help you determine if a conversation with me would be worthwhile: It's my deep personal mission to share my expertise so I can transform the businesses and lives of business owners. Additionally, my experience growing an international consulting firm provided me a tremendous amount of insight and experience. I would love to share that insight and experience with you.

Here are some testimonials of other people who think I'm worth the investment:
<Half page of testimonials.>

I look forward to speaking with you.

Best,
Bob

Bob Gatsby, CEO, Gatsby Strategies

<Links to Email, LinkedIn, Phone
Long tagline about how the company strives and succeeds at being the very best.>

P.S. Here are more testimonials. *Really, I'm that good.*

Coroner's Report: As over the top as Bob's email may seem, the mistake of focusing on oneself (the seller) instead of making it about the recipient (the buyer) is one of the most common sales communication errors. The vast majority of sales emails fatally start with some form of the word "I." Yes, even yours, dear reader. If I were a betting gal, I'd put money on you having more than one email in your recent sent items that starts with "I'm..." after the greeting.

For Bob, that's just the beginning. First of all, his email is just too damn long. With all of the testimonials, it took up twice as much real estate in my inbox than what you see here. You'll learn why less is more when we get to The Overwhelmer.

Bob's opening statement, "I've been meaning to..." seems to indicate that I've been on Bob's mind for some time. He's just been so very busy, he hasn't had a chance to act on his rumination. Call me cynical, but I don't believe Bob. He probably says that to all his prospects. He's not alone, as this strategy is pretty common. It might be genuine when there is an existing relationship. However, it would be a little odd for me to stay on the mind of someone who has only known me over LinkedIn for a hot second. I mean, I do try to make an impression, but Bob is definitely pushing it here. Regardless of your offering, you are in the business of trust. Skepticism about your sincerity at this early stage doesn't bode well.

After the initial niceties, Bob points out that he wouldn't usually stoop so low as to reach out to a meager prospect personally. He has people for that. He then makes a vague reference to my profile, while making zero connection to what prompted his outreach.

Instead of making me feel special, it feels fake and condescending. I just don't believe you care about anyone but yourself, Bob. I'm already imagining a conversation with Bob where he talks over me for a half-hour, spewing forth more words that sound a lot like this email, finally finishing with something akin to the old line, "Well enough about me. What do you think about me?"

It's too bad Bob doesn't know that how he makes people feel is way more important than anything he says. This will be addressed further in later examples. Feelings are the *most* important thing in sales. Reading Bob's email makes me feel like I want to hit the delete button and move on with my life. Without Bob.

Like most salespeople, Bob probably has good intentions. Though it's a bit of an afterthought, he specifically mentions his deep mission to help others. It... could be true. (Ya never know.) He may simply be trying to appear impressive, interesting, and credible so that he'll get a response. In his mind, if his prospects know the benefits and value of working with him, they have to say yes. How could they resist?! Bob also believes that name dropping and adding lots of testimonials from others will make his case even more compelling. Spoiler alert: It doesn't.

What Bob isn't keeping in mind is that his prospects don't actually care about him. If they cared at all, they stopped caring after the first paragraph. If they stopped reading altogether, that might actually be a good thing. By focusing on tooting his own horn rather than focusing on something that is of actual interest to the prospect, Bob is completely missing the opportunity to create a connection. Bob is that guy at the party who talks too loudly and brags about himself while anyone who comes into contact with him makes fake eye contact with a lamp on the other side of the room, gets away as fast as possible, and avoids him for the rest of the evening by any means possible. Oh look, cheese cubes!

Still, the urge to highlight positive attributes and proselytize about one's own value is one that many business builders find hard to resist.

Advice for Resuscitation: Resist. Don't be like Bob. Start auditing your emails for ego words. Emails that start with some form of the word "I" immediately convey to the receiver that you care more about your goals than theirs. Edit most sentences that start with I, We, Our, or the name of your company. Whenever possible, start with You or Your. It's a free filter you can use to instantly bring life to all of your sales communications.

For example, "Your LinkedIn profile indicates that you have a reputable sales training practice that helps small to midsize organizations..."

If you want to use the word "I" for good instead of evil, follow it by "I noticed that..." or "I'm curious to know...." so that it quickly transforms from being about you to being about them.

Knowing what to ask is always more important than knowing what to say.

The second phrase, "I'm curious to know..." is especially useful. In a recent interview, someone asked me what I'd look for as the number one quality when hiring a salesperson. The answer is... drum roll please... curiosity. Knowing what to ask is always more important than knowing what to say. It's one of the reasons that scripted sales training doesn't work well. It's also why all of my training focuses on principles instead of scripts. Even reading this book, you may be thinking, "Just tell me what to say."

Here's the deal: You're not a robot, and you're not putting messages on billboards. You're a human being with the job of building a connection with another human being. Curiosity is an essential human quality that will serve you well as a business builder. It's also the key to not being The Egomaniac. The other problem with scripted sales language is that even if you memorize your lines perfectly, the prospect doesn't get a copy of the script. Great sales is more like skillful improvisation. Preparation, confidence, and experience all help. The more of each, the better. Still, anyone can be reasonably successful out of the gate if they have the right attitude and approach.

As the saying goes, "Be interested, not interesting." Instead of making statements about yourself, ask questions about them.

For example, "I'm curious to learn more about what makes your training unique and how you share that message with the world. Would you be open to sharing your approach with me?"

When tempted to name drop and add testimonials, only do so if there's a direct connection to your prospect. While ten quotes from people they've never heard of is less than useless, one quote or reference from someone they know and respect may hold some weight. Similarly, mentioning a huge global company you've worked with means nothing unless your prospect is also a big global company. Anytime you use references or testimonials, you want the prospect to see something of themselves in those positive experiences.

Egomaniac Example 2:

Subject: Our new Pilot Program

Dear Charlene,

I stumbled on your website and wanted to connect virtually.

We are a small but growing agency helping companies like yours generate more leads and customers with our proprietary strategies.

Our clients include several Fortune 500 companies as well as these others: *<list of fancy companies>*

I am reaching out because we're testing a new offer that might be of interest to you. We're not sure quite yet if this new program make sense for us at scale, so we are trying it out on a small group of clients in a Pilot Program.

I would love to demonstrate this exciting new offer. I'm available next Tuesday if there's a time that works for you that day?

Thanks,
Elizabeth

Coroner's Report: Now that you're tuned into the ego words, they should jump off the page at you. For many of my clients and students, this awareness is the first step to bringing new life to all future sales emails. You're welcome.

In this new case, it's particularly easy because literally every paragraph starts with I, We, or Our. Similar to Bob's email and many others I've received, there's a generic reference to my website. Both Bob and Elizabeth used similar openers with "coming across" and "stumbling on" me as a potential prospect. Does this mean they were originally shopping for weight loss supplements, but then tripped over my information instead? Or, were they doing random keyword searches in Google, or Sales Navigator queries in LinkedIn?

The complete focus on themselves makes me question if they've taken the time to look me up at all. The generic phrase "companies like yours" makes me think not. It's the one place where Elizabeth could have made some small connection, and she failed.

Possibly worse than making it all about herself, Lizzy here tells me things she shouldn't. "Small but growing" may be exciting for her company, but only tells me that they are in super sales mode. I'm picturing a giant sales goal thermometer poster on their office wall and the promise of a trip to Sedona when they color it in all the way to the top. Go team Lizzy! Without me.

"I'm reaching out because..." is a phrase that's actually not fatal. Sometimes it helps to explain your motivation. That said, no prospect wants to be your guinea pig. Especially when what you're testing is the validity of your own business model.

The final nail in the coffin is the one/two punch of "I would love to…" with the call to action (question mark) to respond within her precious window of availability. *Sigh.*

Advice for Resuscitation: In addition to everything you changed after meeting poor Bob, shift your perspective around any frequent use of the words "I would like to…" and "I would love to…" Of course you would love to share your offerings. Of course you would like to get a meeting. The question is why do your prospects want to talk to *you?*

Never make your quota or your dream or your boss's expectations their problem. They don't know you well enough to care. Instead, create a genuine connection between something you know about them and something they actually care about. The thing they care about most is their own business. Focus on what makes them come alive. It's not about you. Stick a post-it note to your computer screen that says, "It's not about me" or write it 100 times on your whiteboard. Whatever you need to do. Instead of telling them you're reaching out to talk about how fabulous you are, show them that you come from a place of curiosity and service. The only way you can ever provide authentic and meaningful value is to start conversations with the focus on those you wish to serve.

There's a hidden selfish motivation here that I do encourage: Shocking though it may seem, you may not want them as a customer. Sales is about building relationships. As in other areas of life, not everyone is a perfect match. It may take time and experience for you to identify ideal compatibility.

Imagine throwing yourself at the shiniest person at the party and giving them all your best dance moves, only to find out that, as much as they want you…. you don't want them. They never let you lead, they're cheap, and their breath reeks of scope creep. Meanwhile, your soulmate is still out there somewhere. Worse, you've wasted so much time being a show-off to incompatibles that your soulmate has moved on.

Instead, open the connection with something specific about them that indicates there could be a match. This may be a trusted connection you share, a group that you both belong to, a specific offering of theirs, or an ideal customer they target. Again, always lead with something about them, not about you.

Always lead with something about them, not about you.

From there, consider the earlier advice and use a phrase like, "I'm curious to learn more about...." instead of "I would love to..."

Alternatively, you can pose a question that demonstrates your curiosity and paves the way for conversation. Phrase it in a way that makes them want to answer in the affirmative. Specifically, take away any intention on your part to invite them to your dog and pony show. For example, "Would you be open to a conversation to delve a bit deeper into your training methodology and ideal client? If time allows, I can also answer any questions you may have about me and then we can mutually decide on next steps, if any."

The last part of that phrase, "...then we can mutually decide on next steps, if any" is a great reincarnator, and one you will want to use often. Like I always tell my kids who are both teenagers now: In any relationship, you want to find the right person and be the right person. Be careful that you're not trying so hard to impress a potential partner or friend that you forget what's going to make you happy as well. When you approach a potential business partner with the clear and genuine intention to establish a mutual fit, it will feel better to both of you. Starting this way, you establish greater trust from the start and make your potential future together that much stronger.

Egomaniac Example 3:

Subject: Business Solutions

Hi,

My name is Kevin, and I'm the VP of Business Development at Up in Ashes Enterprises. My previous email may have missed you, so I wanted to try again.

We are the leading provider of business solutions for speakers and consultants. I would love to tell you more about what we do and see if you might be interested in our services.

Please click on this link to schedule a Zoom call with me. I look forward to speaking to you!

Regards,
Kevin
VP of Business Development
Up in Ashes Enterprises

Coroner's Report: My ninth-grade English teacher, Mrs. Hallall, used to write corrections on our papers in red ink. She called it "bleeding" on our work. The more red ink, the worse the grade. If I were to follow Mrs. Hallall's practice on Kevin's email, I'd be bleeding all over this thing. First, we cross out most instances of my, I, we, and our. We can cross out him telling us his name and company name since I can see that information quite clearly in at least two other places as soon as I get his email. His title is also redundant. In fact, most prospects don't care what your title is at this stage, and leading with it here just puts a spotlight on the fact that Kevin is a sales professional. "Hey look at me! I have a quota to meet, and this stuff isn't going to sell itself!"

Next, we have to kill the sentences that start with, "I wanted to..." and "I would love to..." And finally, let's address the call to action around setting a meeting.

Kevin does get points for keeping his email short, and ending with a request for a call. In most cases, your goal early on is simply that: Get a first meeting. More on that when we get to The Overwhelmer in Chapter 3. That said, Kevin is taking a big risk by assuming anyone is going to click his link to take the lead in finding a mutually acceptable time to meet. In a recent casual poll of my fellow National Speakers Association members on Facebook, there was a fairly wide range of reactions to the "click my scheduling link" approach. A few stated they liked the convenience, but tended to be more open to the idea past the initial stages of contact. On the other side, there were several people who stated that being asked to click a link to schedule would be grounds for an immediate delete. No way, no how.

The closing exclamation, "I look forward to speaking with you soon!" in combination with everything else, translates to a more likely, "I look forward to speaking at you soon!" No thanks.

There's a saying: How things start is how they go. This is only a three-paragraph email, yet it conveys almost zero interest in me, my business, my needs, my goals, or anything other than The Kevin Show. If Kevin doesn't care about prioritizing me now, why would I have reason to believe he would ever prioritize me as a customer. Clearly, Kevin just wants to talk about Kevin. Kevin, that's what therapy is for. Thanks, I'm all set.

Advice for Resuscitation: Before hitting send on any email, bleed all over it. Find and change anything that will make you seem like an Egomaniac. Even though your prospect won't specifically know these rules, they will subconsciously be thinking the things being pointed out here. Make your targets feel that they are more important and more interesting to you than you.

In addition to the advice from the other examples, you can use verbiage along the lines of, "There may come a time in our ongoing discussions when you become interested in how we help speakers and consultants with critical backoffice solutions. Right now, getting to know you better and earning your trust is the priority. The first step is to learn more about your business and goals."

In asking for a meeting, be sure to show your prospect that you respect their time. Provide a specific length for the call, a high-level agenda, an assurance that you are not going to talk at them the whole time, and a soft close on future next steps.

Here's an example of doing all of these things in just a couple of sentences: Understanding that your time is at a premium, let's start with a 30-minute call. Certainly, we can answer any immediate questions you may have as well, and then we can mutually decide on next steps, if any.

In terms of the logistics for scheduling the meeting, there are varied opinions on this as stated earlier. I'm someone who does appreciate the potential convenience of a scheduling link when positioned correctly. Therefore, I typically advise giving two options of different days and times along with the offer to use their link (if they have one) or yours, whichever is easier for them. Remember that people operate on packed schedules these days, so be realistic in your timing. I've learned that it's almost never a great idea to request a meeting within the same week. Imagine yourself in front of the calendar of your prospect, and suggest options that are at least a week or two weeks out.

Here's the other dynamic to consider in all of this: If you position yourself as having a wide open schedule with all the availability in the world, how successful does that make you sound? If you're not a *little* busy serving your current clients, are you really that good? Find the balance that portrays you as successful and busy, while also having flexibility and bandwidth to take on new clients and serve them well.

An example word track that you may draw inspiration from is: Are you available next Thursday <month/day> at 10am or the following Tuesday <month/day> at 3:30pm EDT? If neither of these times work, please let me know your availability and we can coordinate from there.

2

RIP — The Apologizer

Cause of Death: Fear and lack of confidence (aka head trash)

Primary Symptoms of The Apologizer:

- Any opening phrase that sounds apologetic
- Using words such as bothering, bugging, pestering, annoying, etc.
- Egomaniac symptoms rooted in deep insecurity
- Asking for too little in the call to action, or no call to action at all
- Anything that sounds like, "Please don't hate me, but..."

Apologizer Example Email 1

Subject: Sorry, me again!

Hi Charlene,

It's me, Farley, again! Sorry to bother you. I really hate to be that annoying guy who makes you sigh or cringe every time you hear from me.

Still, I wanted to reach out one last time to see if I can get 15 minutes of your time to demonstrate how my company can help you with your recruiting challenge? I promise to be brief. Can we please set up a quick call?

Thanks so much,
Farley

Coroner's Report: The Apologizer is one of the most common sales personas. The Farley of the world are typically either solopreneurs or very junior salespeople. I'm guessing that this Farley is in his 20s, working his first sales job out of college, and in way over his head. He knows it, too. Someone hired him with grand promises of fat commission checks and being part of growing something. Farley probably dresses up for work even though he doesn't have to, and has really good hair. Like all apologizers, he worries a lot about what others think of him. As friends, apologizers are usually awesome. They tend to be high achievers who want to do good things for the world and prefer to keep things positive. As business builders, they need a lot of coaching. Luckily, their language makes Apologizers pretty easy to spot. As in the game of poker, salespeople have tells. Apologizing for bothering, bugging, or being a pest is one of the most obvious mindset tells you'll see.

This email also suffers from overuse of ego words, which is another tell. Unlike the Egomaniac, it comes from lack of confidence rather than self-centeredness. In fact, it is Farley's empathy for his prospect that's making him work against his own efforts. Apologizers will often say things such as, "Well, I know how much I hate getting sales calls!"

Taking this a step further, Farley pretty much states that he hates his job. Oh, if you ask him in person while he's at the office, he will say he *loves* his job and is *so* excited about being part of a growing team, *yada yada, yada.* Still, his email betrays the truth. Farley doesn't want to be in sales. As much as he likes the idea of those big commission checks, his true perception of "sales" is being that annoying guy who makes people display obvious distaste.

Because he perceives the whole process as painful and annoying for everyone involved, he's using a lot of language that attempts to offset this harsh inner reality. In addition to overtly apologizing for reaching out at all, there are some more subtle clues which are typical. For example, The Apologizer will often use a question mark at the end of a statement, even though it's not actually a question. For example, "Still, I wanted to reach out one last time to see if I can get 15 minutes of your time to demonstrate how my company can help you with your recruiting challenge?" This will come up again with The Corny Cornball and The Defeatist.

Farley also only dares to ask for a 15-minute call. To further stress how much he appreciates being given even the slightest consideration, he again promises to be brief and uses his very best manners to the end. I can imagine Farley using the same tone when he asked his parents if he could borrow their car that morning. Again. *Sigh. Cringe.*

Advice for Resuscitation: It may seem like the obvious advice is, "Stop apologizing." However, that would be like telling someone who is trying to lose weight to just stop eating cupcakes. Unless you change their mindset, the behavior probably isn't going to change. We must address the emotions at play. The real work that The Apologizer needs to do here is primarily internal.

Before sending another email, first come to terms with why you think selling is inherently painful for both the seller and the buyer. Where did this belief come from? For example, perhaps Farley has had some bad interactions as a customer or often heard his parents talk about awful sales experiences. To shift that perception, instead think about what an exciting opportunity this is for you to create a different experience for both you and your future clients. How awesome! The true power of sales is the opportunity to save people from their problems and make the world a better place. You get to be the hero. If you're Farley, you *want* to be a hero.

Stop trying to protect your prospects from you. They need you.

It's okay to want your prospects to like you. In fact, it's important that they do. You just want them to like you for the right reasons. Stop trying to protect your prospects from you. They need you.

Take the time to fully internalize *why* they need you. Get crystal clear on the value of your business and solution set. If you're new to a company or in a sales role, insist that you get the proper onboarding. While it's obviously important for you to be an expert in whatever you're selling, it's even more important for you to be an expert in the type of people you're calling. Role-play being in your ideal customer's shoes. Understand their world in detail, and feel their pain. What are they experiencing that you are in a unique position to solve? What's the urgency for them to get the help they need as soon as possible?

When you reach out, it should be with feelings of confidence, excitement, and hope. Instead of picturing your prospect sighing and cringing, imagine them smiling and thinking, "Thank goodness you reached out. I've been struggling with this very thing!"

In addition, get over your head trash telling you attempting to reach someone multiple times makes you a bad person. People are busy. Life happens. On average, it takes between 7 - 12 touches to get a deal. Again, remember that you are reaching out to people who need you. You'd be doing them a disservice if you didn't keep trying.

If you have reached out a few times and feel the need to justify your repeated outreach, you can say something like, "The reason for my professional persistence is that..."

In Farley's case as a recruiter, he might have replaced the apology with, "The reason for my professional persistence is that advisory firms such as yours often struggle to scale growth when the owner is filling every role in the company."

He would then ask if I'd be open to a conversation where he could learn more about my long-term business goals, see if mapping out a future hiring plan made sense, and then mutually agree on next steps, if any. If needed, in a subsequent message Farley could highlight that even if I'm not looking to hire additional headcount right now, there may be some helpful information he can share to make that process easier when the time is right. Lead with confidence and end with confidence. Only use question marks when you have a question.

Finally, never ever ask for only 15 minutes as a first meeting. Not only does it diminish the value of having a conversation with you, it is disrespectful to the other person as well. All first meetings should have a primary goal of getting to know more about your prospect. If you're only willing to dedicate 15 minutes towards that endeavor, you can't be truly interested in building a relationship with them. Skip the speed dating.

Apologizer Example Email 2

Subject: Just following up...

Dear Charlene,

I'm just following up to see if you have 5 - 10 minutes free anytime this week? If so, I would like to talk to you about how I can help redesign your website. Don't worry - I'm not expensive!

Think about it. If I can't convince you in less than 10 minutes, we'll pretend we never spoke and I'll never bother you again.

If you're not interested, I understand.

Just let me know.
Kind Regards,
Martha

Coroner's Report: Martha asked me to think about it and let her know. Like most prospects, I will never let her know. This moment of silence for poor Martha is going to be long. So long. Oddly, Martha somehow manages to be apologetic throughout the entire email without ever actually saying the word "sorry."

The phrase, "I'm just following up..." may as well start with, "Please don't hate me as much as I hate myself right now..." Martha is not only minimizing her own value, she's betraying her real fear of rejection. She's not alone. This tendency to shrink back isn't The Apologizer's fault.

"I'm just following up..." (IJFU) is a lesion on your sales communications. IJFU seems benign at first. When you dig into it though, you find that it's only a surface symptom of something much deeper. It's a sign of deep programming that has been etched in your brain, probably from a very young age. You are so afraid of rejection that you reject yourself before a new prospect has a chance to.

Starting with that phrase is an admission of secret guilt. In her head, Martha is imagining me opening her email and thinking with a scowl on my face, "What the heck does Martha want now? Why is she bothering me?!" To which she is virtually putting up her hands *ala*, "I come in peace!"

On some level, she must believe she can convince me to work with her if only I'd give her the chance. Again, poor Martha. She believes that her job is to convince people. In her mind, she's a professional arm twister. Even if she *is* skilled at getting a few people to give her company a chance, it has to feel awful. No wonder she's an Apologizer. It's also why she lets me off the hook so easily. She's probably relieved not to hear back from me.

Advice for Resuscitation: Eliminate the IJFU phrase from all future communications. If it helps you change the habit, imagine that instead of "I'm Just Following Up," IJFU actually stands for "I Just F'ed Up." Ok, maybe not. Kidding aside, we do want to be careful not to feed the 'not good enough' monster that's already living in your head.

After following the advice given after Farley's terrible email, it's time to face your fears. Fear is an adaptive behavior. That is, almost all fear is learned. Biologically, humans across the globe are only born with two innate fears: fear of loud noises and fear of falling. Although the second one may be accurately described as a fear of being dropped, it's not about rejection.

Fear is an adaptive behavior.

Take a moment right now to write out exactly what you fear about reaching out to potential customers. What is it that causes you to go into fight or flight mode; specifically, flight? Get beyond thinking about how your sales-related fear *feels* for you, to what it *means* for you. Your immediate response might be, "I don't know." You may look at the blank piece of paper and feel a bit overwhelmed. This is normal. Whatever fears you have, you learned them as a survival mechanism. Your deepest instinct will be to hold them sacred; to protect them so they continue to serve you.

Here's the truth about rejection: Some people are going to tell you no. Sometimes no means "not right now" and sometimes it actually means, "I need you to help me say yes." Chris Voss, author of *Never Split the Difference: Negotiating As If Your Life Depended On It* offers the best advice: "Every stated objection is a counter-offer in disguise, an implied agreement and cry for help. The stated objection isn't the real problem. It's blocking for an emotional one."

On the surface, objections may feel like rejection. It may take some practice to get great at figuring out when a prospect is really crying out for help. Your goal should be to get to a place with your prospects that when their no really means no, you agree with them. Sometimes it's really not a good mutual fit. When that's the case, no is the right answer. There's no need to fear it.

Meanwhile, take all of the advice given to The Egomaniac. Focus on your prospect instead of yourself. Make it about them. When your ask is to get time with someone to learn about them, and they say no, they're not rejecting you. They're rejecting the opportunity to talk about themselves. You'll find that people are usually pretty happy to talk about themselves. The key is for them to believe that that's the real agenda.

You also need to be clear about your goal. Your goal is to make a connection and schedule a conversation. If it makes sense, then you'll have more conversations, determine mutual fit, and perhaps discuss options for working together.

Many business builders experience almost paralyzing fear because, like Martha, they think they have to be great at *convincing* others to do things. Not only is that a lot of pressure, it's wrong. Take a breath and give yourself a break. You don't have to do ANY selling right now, beyond getting the first conversation. In that first conversation, the prospect should be the one doing most of the talking. You just need to be genuinely interested, really listen,

When you truly believe in your own value, you'll never worry about "bothering" anyone again.

ask great questions, and take notes so you don't have to remember stuff you will need later. Relax. You got this.

Back to the advice about Farley's email, all of this requires that you truly, madly, deeply believe in the value you are bringing to the table. People need you! Even though you are going to start by focusing on the prospect instead of selling your own value, it's absolutely critical that you go into every interaction with that deep sense of value in your heart. When you truly believe in your own value, you'll never worry about "bothering" anyone again.

3

RIP — The Overwhelmer

Cause of Death: Way too much, way too soon

Primary Symptoms of The Overwhelmer:

- Sharing too much information
- Long bulleted lists
- Run-on sentences with faulty grammar and too much punctuation
- Multiple links and attachments
- Pricing details
- Sending multiple emails with the same information
- Anything that sounds like, "But wait… there's more!!!"

Special note: Because Overwhelmers are notorious for ridiculously long messages, the emails below have been truncated as noted. You can imagine one of those reality television scenes where they have to time lapse someone's blind date while they talk... and talk... and talk. Goodness knows I barely wanted to read these wordy things in their entirety. You sure don't.

Overwhelmer Example Email 1

Subject: hi Charlene , It's Rod Walker!

Charlene

How have you been? Per my voicemail, I wanted to personally reach out to you and share with you what I'm doing these days and why I am so excited! As you probably remember, I was *<emotional description of prior job, company, and responsibilities.>*

I have to say, this past summer was surreal for me as I was so busy with *<lots of words that are strung together in such a meaningless way, that it's almost like he messing with me.>*

OK, now that we walked down memory lane, let me share with you what I have been up to the past 5 years and why am I more excited than I have been in the past 20 years of my career in the space that I am working within? Well, at my old company the main reason I had the record-breaking success I enjoyed *<winning lots of awards such as this one and that one>* was because *<long dissertation about core values and how that helped his clients on both a "corporate and professional level." A bunch of statistics that mean literally nothing to me.>* The problem with the traditional sales process *<goes on to bash his prior company>* This always use to frustrate me since my whole philosophy was *<exactly what he already described earlier in the email.>*

Needless to Say my current Company has cracked the code of *<doing a whole bunch of stuff that might be impressive if I worked in that space and/ or had any interest whatsoever.>*

Here are some of the benefits that our clients get when they work with us in addition to excellent service from people they can rely on and trust:

- Bullet
- Bullet
- Bullet
- Bullet
- Thank goodness these aren't real bullets

My promise to you is if you give me the opportunity to help you and your business (or referred me to someone) I won't waste your time! Please do me a favor and click the link below to schedule a time for you and I to meet up or jump on a quick call and identify areas we can possibly help. In the meantime, check out our website and our YouTube channel. I've also attached our pitch deck and one-pager so you can see more before we talk.

Thanks so much, I'm so excited to connect!

Rod

Rod Walker
Managing Partner
ZOMBI, Inc
<8 lines of contact information>
<more links>

Coroner's Report: Overwhelmers are Egomaniacs with the opposite problem of Apologizers. They are SO EXCITED (!!!) about what they do and believe in it SO MUCH (!!!) that they can't help but electronically vomit over anyone with an email address. And *oy,* the exclamation marks. Overwhelmers love exclamation marks!! They don't mean any harm. They're like puppies; so excited for human interaction that they can't help but jump around, knocking things over with their wagging tail, and drooling all over the place. They crave attention, and may experience manic episodes where they can't figure out why everyone else isn't as excited as they are. Overwhelmers cause other people to feel overwhelmed, and they are also the most likely to feel overwhelmed. It's the least sustainable of all the personas. Nobody can maintain this level of volume, particularly in the absence of a positive feedback loop.

As is typical for Overwhelmer emails, the most obvious issue with this particular email is that it's just too damn long. Remembering the saying "how things start is how they go," I would never reply to this guy. If he's like this over email, I can only imagine what special torture a phone call with him would be like. While I appreciate the positive energy and passion, ain't nobody got time for that. Another thing to consider is that the majority of business emails are opened on mobile devices; between 55% - 75%, depending on the study. That's a lot of scrolling and squinting. Furthermore, if I wasn't overwhelmed or stressed out before I read his email, I am now. On top of the time commitment Rod is asking me to make with the email message itself, he has included links and attachments. Even putting potential security risks aside, that's a lot to ask.

The other thing that makes this email almost unreadable is that he has prioritized his own stream of consciousness over cogent and correct sentences. Overwhelmers tend to rush and make a lot of mistakes. There's just so much to share with so many people. Who has time to proofread??

Mistakes in sentence structure, grammar, and spelling probably won't be fatal as an occasional occurrence. If you get a prospect who won't do business with you only because you put a semicolon in the wrong place or missed a *Damn You Autocorrect!* moment, they probably aren't a client you want anyway. However, it is possible to kill a deal with a complete lack of attention to detail in combination with overwhelming tone, too-long length, oversharing of external materials, and general wordiness. And exclamation points!!!!! Am I right?!

Advice for Resuscitation: As a confession, I'm a recovering Overwhelmer. Therefore, I truly do appreciate what it's like to love what you do so much that it's hard to contain your excitement. While it is also possible to overwhelm someone with energy, live interaction gives you an opportunity to be perceptive in real time and adjust accordingly. You can feel when you're talking too much and apply one of my favorite sales acronyms: W.A.I.T. It stands for Why Am I Talking? Write it on a post-it and stick it on your computer screen.

For emails, the best advice I ever got was equally simple: Use less words.

Using fewer words isn't just an exercise in editing. As is almost always the case, it requires a shift in mindset and approach. Like The Egomaniac, remember that it's not about you. It's about the people you serve. As long as you don't scare your prospect off at this stage by being way too extra, you will get a chance to reveal your value, passion, and commitment. You just have to earn the right to do that. In the meantime, find and maintain a more elegant energy level. Change most of your exclamation marks to periods. Question marks work, too, as long as you're actually asking a question. Assume your email will be read on a mobile device, and format it in a way that is easy to read on a small screen.

As advised to The Apologizer, also focus on the right goal. Rod's email was fine if his goal was to catch me up on how he spent his summer, the changes to his resume, and his philosophy on life and business. That is, if we were old friends and I actually cared about his life. If his goal was to get the very first conversation with me, he overshot it by many miles.

Your first goal is to make a connection and schedule a conversation.

It bears repeating: Your first goal is to make a connection and schedule a conversation. If it makes sense, then you'll have more conversations, determine mutual fit, and perhaps discuss options for working together. Don't use email to have the entirety of your side of the conversation. You won't get the other side.

Also, switch to decaf.

Overwhelmer Email Example #2

Subject: Working together

Warm Greetings!

I hope this email reaches you in good health and high spirits!

Quick Question: Have you thought about using LinkedIn to generate sales meetings?

The reason for my question is that we have seen great results helping companies like yours get more contacts and generate a LOT more business. Here's how we do it!! *<Here is a long, detailed, step-by-step process that they probably consider proprietary.>* I've attached some additional information so you'll have it handy for your own reference as well as to share with others! You can also get view much of this information (and more!) at this link.

Unlike other companies who charge thousands of dollars in consulting fees, we also have a subscription model that is only $97 per month! Or, you can sign up for the full year and get a discounted price of $997. If that sounds like a CRAZY great deal, it's because it is!! We also have performance-based, quarterly, and multi-year plans. Our results are proven and guaranteed!!! You will get SO much more business that what we are charging!! However, our main mission is to help businesses like yours become more successful, If you have awesome results, we know that you will recommend us to others! It's a win-win!! Here are some of the other reasons that we consistently outperform every other lead gen company out there:

- *Bullet about technology being special*
- *Bullet about people being special*
- *Bullet about service being special*

Here's a testimonial from one of customers who DOUBLED the number of leads they were getting each month, just by working with us!!! I would love to set up a quick call to find out what you're doing now and how we can help you get MUCH better results! Are you available on any of these days or times to meet? This week: Thursday at 9am, 11am or 4pm. Or, Friday anytime between 10am - 4pm. Next week: Monday 10am - 2pm; Tuesday anytime EXCEPT 11am; Wednesday between 10am - 1pm or after 3pm; Thursday at 9am; or Friday anytime between 11am - 4pm EXCEPT 1:30pm - 2:30pm.

We can meet up for coffee or lunch, or do a video call. Or, a regular phone call works too! Whatever is easiest for you!!

In addition, we have a free webinar coming up that I think you will find very helpful. Here is the link for that if you want to check it out!

Looking forward to it!!

Dakota

<Name>

<Title>

<Email>

<Three phone numbers>

<Fax number>

<Website>

<Physical address>

<Four lines of social media>

<Logo graphic>

<QR code>

<Tagline>

<Photo>

<Awards>

<Morse code>

<Smoke signal pattern>

Coroner's Report: Despite a few creative liberties, this is classic Overwhelmer oversharing and pretty darn close to one sitting in my Future Clients folder right now. As with most of these examples, these salespeople think they are doing a good thing. In the mind of the Overwhelmer, they are luring the prospect with data, differentiators, benefits, and flexibility. The truth is they are pushing the prospect away. It's way too much information, way too soon. They are really creating a no-win scenario. Prospects aren't likely to read a long-winded, overwhelming email, particularly if it's cold outreach. Even if the information-vomit email was prompted by some initial interest, there's another problem — because Dakota has emailed all of the information that I need to know, including all the "special sauce," I have no real reason to talk to them. I can file the information away for "when the time is right" along with any information I've received from competitors. When I'm ready to seriously consider which solution to use, it's unlikely I will go back to the files. Instead, someone completely new will get me to have a conversation, create an emotional connection, and earn my trust.

The barrage of too much muchness (yes that's a word; ask the Mad Hatter) includes overwhelming me with options. Though most people wouldn't commit this offense in so many ways, Dakota's email demonstrates the common potential pitfalls.

In this example, Dakota gave me at least three choices for getting more information, four or five pricing options, four ways to meet, and a list of potential meeting times that could create a tesseract. We will address why you should never lead with pricing, in Chapter 8 - The Order Taker. For now, just know that Dakota messed up. Providing some choice is beneficial to creating buy-in. Too many options… not so much.

In his 2004 book, *The Paradox of Choice: Why More is Less,* Barry Schwartz wrote about how too many options lead to anxiety, indecision, paralysis, and dissatisfaction. I've seen this to be true throughout my sales career as well. Regardless of published data, tune into how you feel when you are faced with long lists of options, particularly several in one email. It feels overwhelming, right? Being overwhelmed is stressful, and stress creates a fight-or-flight reaction. Hitting the delete button is the quickest way to satisfy a flight response.

Despite the well-intentioned offer to do "whatever is easiest," Dakota is making the whole interaction much more difficult. Confused people don't buy.

Confused people don't buy.

This is also a good example to call your attention to signature blocks. More lines after a sender's sign-off actually equals *less* credibility. This may surprise some people since it's so contrary to the intent. At this stage, too many lines of miscellaneous information comes across as self-absorbed and frivolous. Some of it is downright distracting and outdated. Maybe I should fax Dakota and let them know how much I hated their email.

While The Egomaniac and The Overwhelmer are most likely to abuse the space below their goodbye, it's a virus that anyone can catch. Some companies even give it to their employees by mandate.

Advice for Resuscitation: The signature block is an ideal place to reinforce the best overall advice for The Overwhelmer: Less is more. Put yourself in the shoes of the person you are emailing. What will inspire them to build a first-level connection? Focus on this specific stage of the relationship. You want them to agree to a first date. That's it. There's no need to give them your login information for Ancestry.com, all of your medical records, and a copy of the Spelling Bee Award you won in fourth grade.

Go through each line in your signature and consider: Why does this particular prospect need or want this information right now?

In some industries, awards or certifications are critical. In others, it comes off as a little ridiculous. If your full name appears in other places on the email, you don't need to include it again. If they can hit Reply and see your email address, leave it out. Unless your prospect is likely to drive a DeLorean back to 1997, don't include a fax number. If they don't need it, delete it.

Here's a technology tip: Almost all email programs will allow you to save multiple versions of your signature block. The one you use for your earliest connection with someone may not be the same as the reply you are sending to a current client. You may want a different email signature for referral partners vs. suppliers. Every bit of real estate on the emails you send is valuable. To push the analogy, it's a buyer's market. Be thoughtful about your buyer, and stage the signature block accordingly. That is, only include the information they need for where they are in the relationship.

All that said, even if you are writing a quick one-sentence reply, always include your direct phone number. There is nothing more frustrating than hunting through old emails to find someone's phone number.

Your job is to solve problems and make your prospects' lives easier. Overwhelmers know this; they just need to resist their natural urge to cover all possible bases at one time. Instead, opt for clarity and brevity. These are your new best friends.

Follow the advice about focusing on the goal of connecting and getting a meeting. Make it about them. If they asked for information, of course you want to give them information. Just send it at the right time, and be extremely careful about emailing it without the benefit of conversation. Live interaction allows you to position any piece of information in a much more meaningful and relevant way. It allows for emotion. It gives you the opportunity to verbally check in on what is resonating and what isn't. When you email information, you leave yourself vulnerable to judgments and objections being formed without you being there to address them.

There is plenty of opportunity for a business builder to talk themselves out of a sale by saying too much. This is especially true for Overwhelmers who can have a tendency to keep talking and introducing new factors after the prospect has agreed to buy. It's one of the things we cover in my training. Still, live human connection is always an advantage. Don't give away your best stuff in an email, when presenting it face-to-face or voice-to-voice provides so many more advantages. Despite the fact that this book is almost totally about email, it is an inferior form of sales communication.

That said, before you share any piece of information at any stage of the sales cycle, you want to know why what they've requested is valuable, who else within the organization will also be looking at it, and specifically how it plays into their decision.

If you're fulfilling a promise to send lots of information, make sure you have a next meeting set with a day and time to review what you will be sending. You may think you're being nice and helpful by sending extra information "just in case." Never electronically vomit all over someone, and especially when they haven't asked for you to reach out. If someone has to scroll to read your email on a full-sized screen, it's too long. On a mobile device, it would be torture.

4

RIP — The Corny Cornball

Cause of Death: Trying to be cute

Primary Symptoms of the Corny:

- Sports analogies or inside jokes
- Any form of poetry
- References to animals or unlikely disasters
- Inspirational quotes, photos, or memes
- Anything that sounds like, "Do you like me? Circle Yes or No"

Corny Cornball Example Email 1

Subject: Don't leave me hangin'

Hello again Charlene,

Julien from Friendly Skills Solutions here. Hope you're having an amazing week filled with so many good things, it's like scoring the winning touchdown at the Super Bowl! Six times!

<PICTURE OF TOM BRADY DOING A TOUCH DOWN>

If you're not feeling that way lately, consider me your new winning wide receiver! I would love the opportunity to connect to share how I can improve your day-to-day in your role as Chief Quarterback for Charlene Ignites, LLC. Even if you're not interested in talking to me or just too busy right now, I'd truly appreciate a quick reply. I'm open!!

Don't leave me hangin'
Julian

Coroner's Report: While my experience is that these Corny Cornball emails usually come from men, women are not immune. Where some men sound like (at best) a buddy from the club or (at worst) a cheesy uncle, women can also come across as too casual or overly familiar. Credibility is at risk in both cases.

Some people might read the first example here and think they wouldn't mind getting this email from Julian. It's not necessarily offensive. Unless, of course, even though I live in New England, I'm secretly a Jets fan. (That would be pure madness of course, not to mention grounds for immediate divorce from my husband of 20+ years, Rob.) Still, Julian is making a risky assumption. Additionally, I still have zero idea why Julian is reaching out or what he can actually do for me. The generic statement, "improve your day-to-day" means nothing to me. There are many other similar statements people use all the time which are equally meaningless, in part because they are now so overused. Some of these include, the generic "increase success," "help you be the best version of yourself," and "help you work ON your business instead of IN your business."

Julian is so busy trying to be witty that he's lost his goal. You'll note that this is a trend among all of these personas. Julian will never get to the end zone because he's playing on the wrong field. Prospects are almost never compelled to give you their valuable time simply because you seem really nice. They won't think, "Hey, I bet this guy would be a blast. I should throw him a bone." In his email, Julian is being cute and funny in the hopes of getting *any* kind of reply. He explicitly says he doesn't care if I want to talk to him or not. He's so starved for attention, that any reaction will do. He's that guy with his hand up to do a high five, as person after person walks by without glancing in his direction, let alone raise their own hand in celebration and comradeship.

Continuing the sports theme, Julian is like Tom Cruise in the movie *Jerry McGuire.* He's reaching out to every loose connection he knows hoping someone, anyone, will give him a shot. Despite Julian's plea, "Don't leave me hangin'..." I just don't see a reason to engage him on any level. If Julian isn't a phone call away from yelling a sweaty, "SHOW ME THE MONEY!!!" into the receiver, he's certainly less than two emails away from being a Defeatist.

Corny jokes are the gateway drug to being icky salesy.

There's also a fine line between The Corny Cornball and The Used Car Salesman who is featured in the next chapter. Corny jokes are the gateway drug to being icky salesy.

Advice for Resuscitation: I'm not telling you to follow the ol' reality television competition mantra, "I'm not here to make friends." In fact, you are. Building relationships is most definitely the goal here. There may even be a point in that friendship when the other person will appreciate, even look forward to, your quirky sense of humor. Now is not that time.

If you're going to start with a fun attempt at making a connection, be sure it's a relevant one. If you see that someone tweets frequently about a specific sport, by all means mention that as something you have in common and connect it to your business. Leverage something personal and real instead of using corny generalizations that are more likely to fall flat. Look at what groups people belong to on LinkedIn and on Facebook if they have a public profile. Read their blog. Follow their tweets. See what they post on Instagram. A lot of salespeople and entrepreneurs complain that social media doesn't help them get business. If this is true for you, it just means you're not leveraging the platforms to their fullest capacity.

Sometimes people in my trainings will ask, "Won't my prospects think I'm stalking them??" If you find a data point that is easily and publicly available online, then mention it as point of similarity, then no. If you hide in the bushes outside their house and mention what you saw them wearing when they got in the car that morning, oh my it is a yes. Hopefully, everyone reading this knows where that line is.

Julian may have scored more points with me by sending an email like:

> "It looks like you and I both tweet a lot about fencing. It's so unusual that I find connections with this shared interest, it piqued my curiosity. Looking at your website, there may be other things we have in common from a business perspective.
>
> Would you be open to a conversation so I can learn more about your services, and further explore these commonalities? I'm happy to answer your questions as well, if you have any.
>
> From there, we can mutually decide if additional conversations make sense and plan accordingly."

No matter what, your first goal is to connect and get to know them. Your relevant and genuine interest in them is going to go a lot further in winning them over than any corny metaphor. If they are going to be your friend, you want it to be real. Remember that there's also a chance that *you* don't want to be *their* friend. Maybe they're a Jets fan.

Corny Cornball Example Email 2

Subject: Don't break my heart, Charlene

Hi Charlene,

Part of me is singing a sad country song for your lack of response which is giving me an achy breaky heart. ⍰

The other part of me is ready to stop bugging you and chase other square dancing partners. :-)

Nevertheless, just going to ask again if there may be any opportunities between your organization and our services?

___ Yes OR ___ No Let me know! ⍰

Regards,
Don

Coroner's Report: It's hard to get much cornier than a country song. If I didn't know this was just a tactic, I'd fear that any conversation with Don will focus largely on his horse, his pickup truck, and the one that got away. If he's sending a lot of these emails, they ALL got away.

What jumps off the page first are all those little boxes with question marks. There are a couple of reasons that those little rascals can show up. In this case, I'm guessing Don used a few cute emojis. My email program apparently hates cute little emojis more than a three-legged dog on an icy pond. So, it just gives me question marks. There's no part of me that is curious to know whether Don was smiling, crying, laughing, or showing me his cool sunglasses. (Though, gosh, I really hope he wasn't trying to give me a hug.) Still, the question marks are poetic. The Corny Cornball has some insecurities.

As discussed in The Apologizer, any reference to bothering or bugging is a mindset tell. The reason why Don is resorting to corny humor is that he is having doubts about the value he brings to my picnic table. In this case, he had already sent me two other emails. One was a more straightforward Overwhelmer / Egomaniac message. I didn't see it as at all relevant to my business, and had no desire to hear Don talk about himself even more, so I didn't reply. The other email was a very odd poem that started with, "Roses are red..." and ended with a confession that he's "no Shakespeare." I know, right?!

Don's example also spotlights another weird trend which is to provide a YES/NO question. My kids sometimes do this when I'm on the phone, i.e. "Can I have ice cream? Circle YES or NO." It's annoying when they do it, and I actually like them. Any verbiage that asks for a yes or no response is also a sign of Order Taker behavior.

If Don believes he can really help me and my business in some way, then persistence is a good thing. Don gets points for not giving up. There are lots of numbers out there about how many touches it takes to get a meeting and close a deal. Most of the data says it's somewhere between 7 - 12. Regardless of source, it's definitely more than two.

The problem is that being a Corny Cornball isn't the right approach. Don's email is about as useful as a trapdoor in a canoe. First of all, let's say I actually was looking for a solution like his but I've just been busy. This does happen, and I have a folder in Outlook where I file such messages. Often, it is the more tenacious person who ultimately gets my business. However, I want to do business with someone who is caring, credible, and professional, not someone who is all foam and no beer.

Advice for Resuscitation: Remember that we are talking about sales emails here, not marketing messages. This is a very important point. Your goal as a sales professional or solo business owner is to make a connection between two people. Even in business-to-business sales, it boils down to one person reaching out to another person. You are seeking one-to-one, two-way communication. The quicker you can get someone from communicating with you online to having a live conversation, the faster you will hit your sales numbers.

Don is resorting to corny tactics now is because he failed with his first email. Instead, do it right the first time. Keep it simple, make it about them, be curious, then ask for a meaningful conversation where you can learn more about each other then mutually decide on next steps, if any. That's it.

> **If email was the most effective path to sales, we wouldn't need salespeople.**

Harsh truth that I often have to share in sales team training is that if email was the most effective path to sales, we wouldn't need salespeople. Companies would just hire really great writers and creative marketers. For a lot of the emails that inspired the ones in this book, I had to reality check whether they were automated or sent from a breathing person with a goal tied to sales instead of marketing. Your biggest advantage in any selling role is that you are human. Be real.

If you are genuinely a creative and slightly corny person, that's totally cool. If you want to really stand out from the crowd, pick up the phone. That alone is rare these days. If you've got cornball tendencies that simply must be expressed, write a country song parody about sales and sing it to me. At least then I know you're a real person. Throughout my sales career, I have been known to sing a few songs and tell a few jokes to my prospects and customers. It can be a risk, and it doesn't always go as planned. Although I will defend against, "TOO JOLLY! BE MORE SERIOUS!" until the day I die, there have been a few other scenes that resulted in solid advice not to quit my day job.

Either way, sending cheesy emails is like kicking a cow turd on a hot day. Everyone's idea of fun is different, but I don't advise it.

Corny Cornball Example 3

Subject: Drowned in a vat of marshmallow?

Charlene!

Either you've drowned in a vat of marshmallow or you're drowning in work. If you have actually drowned in a vat of marshmallow, my deepest sympathy goes out to your family members.

I hate to keep pestering you, but I would love to talk about how much my company can truly help you. Please let me know which one of these things is true and I will proceed accordingly.

_____ Yes, I've drowned in a vat of marshmallow. Please send flowers. (Or grab a stick, some graham crackers and a few chunks of chocolate.)

_____ No, I haven't drowned in a vat of marshmallow, but you may wish I had been, because I have decided I have no interest in your service.

_____ Yes, we have some interest in learning more about your company, but am stuck on some obstacles.

_____ Yes, we have some interest in what you're offering and would like to chat. Call me to set a time for us to meet.

_____ I'm not the right person, please contact __________.

Kind regards,
Stacey Puft

Coroner's Report: Hey, 2014 called and they want their sales email back.

Advice for Resuscitation: Just ... no.

5

RIP — The Used Car Salesman

Cause of Death: Being icky salesy

Primary Symptoms of The Used Car Salesman:

- Numbered surveys that aren't even corny
- Phrases such as "Honestly..." "Frankly..." "To tell you the truth..."
- Overuse of prospect's name
- High-pressure call to action
- Outlandish claims or promises
- Frequent use of spam alert words
- Anything that sounds like, "What can I do to get you into this Prius today?"

Used Car Salesman Example 1

Subject: Just for you, Charlene

Yoohoo Charlene - it's your favorite tech guy again!

Hope you're well! Once again, it's Harry Wormley, V.P. of Business Development at Smokey Technology. Charlene, you're probably thinking, "Who is this guy and why does he keep calling me?" Am I right?

I get it. Just hear me out. Charlene, I feel I would be doing you a disservice if I didn't persist in my efforts to connect with you. Especially since all of our clients have massive results, with a 100% satisfaction rating. You may be wondering, "What is this all about?" Well, that's exactly why I'm reaching out today!

Honestly, I totally understand if you're not in any position to look at how we can help you. If you would just let me know what you would like to do, that would be great. That way, I know how to proceed. I'll make it easy for you. Just reply with 1, 2, 3, or 4.

1. Please keep trying to reach me — I don't care what it takes!
2. Please call me in a few weeks — I want to talk to you but am just busy right now.
3. Please call me in a few months — It's a risk I'm willing to take.
4. Please go away — Give my deal to someone else who wants to have a successful business.

This might help your answer: Since I feel so strongly about our ability to help you, I'm willing to offer you a totally free consultation. This is just for you, and only available for a limited time. Frankly, there's so much value, we just wouldn't be able to offer it to everyone. If you're worried that it's too good to be true, let me set your mind at ease. But, you have to get back to me A.S.A.P.

Thanks Charlene,
Harry

P.S. "Success is not final; failure is not fatal: It is the courage to continue that counts."

— Winston S. Churchill

Coroner's Report: As a disclaimer, I'm using the persona title as an exaggerated movie stereotype. Fair or unfair, The Used Car Salesman conjures up a specific image for most people.

Using a more generic term such as The Salesy Salesperson doesn't create the same visual or more importantly, the same emotional reaction. Of course, there are lots of nice, trustworthy, not-gross used car salesmen in the world. Some of my best friends are used car salesmen. Some of them are women.

Where some of the other personas garner sympathy, The Used Car Salesman can elicit a wide range of reactions from an eye roll to a gag to a, "I'd like to speak to your manager." Even over email, you can just smell their "quota breath."

In this particular episode of *Death of a Used Car Salesman*, Harry left me only one voicemail which hardly qualifies as someone who "keeps calling." I'm happy he did call me (just that once) though because his voice is every bit as *bada-bing, bada-boom* as I'd want it to be for this example. It's perfect. The opening Yoohoo... greeting is also real, which is gratifying for my purpose here and also horrifying. You just can't make this stuff up. I imagine that Harry has quite a collection of cologne and shiny suits. As such, my initial reaction is that Harry makes me want to take a shower. And not in a good way.

You can see this type of salesperson coming a mile away. Interacting with them just feels slimy. The Used Car Salesman thinks he is the World's Greatest Salesperson. They can sell ice to Eskimos. Just ask them.

Harry is making a number of mistakes that are culminating in the visceral *blech* reaction that we have all felt and is hard to describe. Where The Overwhelmer does too much in terms of information and energy, The Used Car Salesman is trying way too hard and using too many "tactics." It feels forced.

For example, while using someone's name is an often-prescribed strategy in sales training, it doesn't translate well to email. It feels like a false and generic tactic. Even worse, most of the time when I get emails like this, my name is in a different font from the rest of the email text. It's obvious they are using a template and just pasting my name in there.

Boasting of "massive results," "limited time offer," and "totally free" screams spam. Not just to me, but to most junk mail filters as well. Your prospect's email provider is giving your email a total score based on a number of factors. For example, you never want to send an email that is one giant image. Using a lot of Used Car Salesman words will also definitely increase your spam score.

In addition to pretty much everything Harry said, here are some examples of other words and phrases that you probably want to avoid:

- Dear Friend
- I promise
- Risk-free
- 100%
- Satisfaction guaranteed
- Act now
- While supplies last

If you Google it, you'll find loads of 100 Words that Trigger Spam lists. Personally, I would never be able to remember not to use 100 words. As an easier rule to remember, avoid anything you'd see on an As Seen on TV commercial.

But wait, there's more!

The response list doesn't work for The Corny Cornball, and it *really* doesn't work in Harry's email. The line on #4, "Give my deal to someone else who wants to have a successful business" borders on The Bridge Burner behavior.

Perhaps the most classic Used Car Salesman move is the use of rhetorical questions. Harry is having an entire conversation with himself. (I'm guessing he's used to this.) Sadly, he thinks he is being incredibly perceptive and empathic by addressing my thoughts and feelings. Meanwhile, I'm not thinking or wondering or worrying about any of the things Harry points out. I wouldn't be thinking of Harry at all except his email is so classic Used Car Salesman.

You may be wondering, "Why is this so annoying?" Well, that's exactly why I wrote this book!

The Used Car Salesman triggers more head trash than any other persona. It's what legit business builders most fear becoming. Rather, what they worry others will perceive them as. When people tell me, "I hate the idea of being icky salesy!" they are thinking of The Used Car Salesman.

In person, these are people who couldn't be more different from Harry. The people with the most Used Car Salesman baggage are genuine, kind-hearted, generous, and naturally curious. Yet, their fear is real and it blocks many of them from doing what they need to do to grow their business. Worse, when they do reach out via email, they end up using a lot of Used Car Salesman tactics! It becomes a self-fulfilling prophecy; a vicious cycle that further cements their negative beliefs about selling, sales, and what it means to be a "salesperson."

Advice for Resuscitation: The Used Car Salesman won't read this or take my advice in any case. The problem with a lot of the Harrys of the world is that they already think they know everything. When I receive cemetery-worthy emails, I usually reply back and ask, "Are you open to some feedback about this email?" It's a simple question. Sometimes the sender will respond, especially if we've had prior contact. Sometimes I cc: the CEO or owner of a business, and the more senior person will reply. More often, I get no response. It's actually a great way to get off sales lists. The Used Car Salesman will almost always send a defensive note back to me. Most commonly, "No. I'm all set."

For everyone else, there are some golden nuggets in here. First, never start an email with the word, Yoohoo. Never ever.

More important is that if you're genuine, kind-hearted, generous, and naturally curious in person, be all that in email, too. No matter what you read in a book or see other "successful" people doing, don't put anything in an email (or a voicemail for that matter) that doesn't feel authentic to who you are as a person. Everything is better when you are more you. Stop worrying about becoming Harry. Your fear is a gremlin. When you say that you hate sales and don't want to be "salesy," you feed your gremlin. Heretofore your gremlin shall be named Harry, and you will no longer feed him. The way to stop feeding Harry is to stop putting so much pressure on yourself. Being Harry is painful. His email is painful. Growing your business shouldn't be painful.

If you're genuine, kind-hearted, generous, and naturally curious in person, be all that in email, too.

Take a breath. Tap into your own core values and remember why you are in business. You are not here to make a quota. You are here to connect with people and help them if there's a good mutual fit for doing so. As my dad used to say, if you're forcing it… you're doing it wrong.

When your Harry Gremlin creeps up in your head, just say, "I see you" and move along. I repeat: Don't feed Harry! Keep your emails short and simple, be genuinely curious and helpful, and focus on making one connection at a time.

As a more tactical note, formatting matters. If you are cutting and pasting your words from one email to the next, or leveraging templates from your CRM system double-check everything before you hit send. To be on the safe side, I always do one last Select All then re-apply a singular font and font size. Also, do a final check for grammar and spelling, including autocorrect. Sanity check your use of spam words. Small things matter. It all adds up.

Used Car Salesman Example 2

Subject: A truly unbelievable offer!

Dear Charlene,

Karl here from Zombee CRM Systems. If you recall, we met at the Coffin Convention back in March. I really enjoyed our conversation where you mentioned that you might be looking for a new CRM system.

Are you all set? Or still looking?

What if I could offer you a way to manage your entire pipeline in a way that is even BETTER than free? What if I could show you a proven system that will actually MAKE you money?

And that's really just the beginning!

But you have to actually talk to me in order for me to share this incredible system with you. What do you say?

I'll give you a call at 2pm on Friday, and you can either hear me out or tell me to go away. I sincerely hope you give me a chance. I promise, you won't regret it. In fact, we literally offer 100% satisfaction.

Looking forward to speaking with you!

Sincerely,
Karl

Coroner's Report: Honestly (to use a common Used Car Salesman phrase), this email was dead on arrival. Even though it's a direct message from someone I met in person, it went directly to my junk folder. Unsurprisingly, I had to dig up a lot of these emails from their salesy graves. In this example, the promise of an "unbelievable deal" in the subject line probably killed it right away. It would have been a painless death, except I decided to read it anyway. In addition, there are several other things that would have led to an unrecoverable spam score. Words like free, incredible, promise, and 100% satisfaction leap off the page if you're a spam junky (or Outlook). Believe it or not, something as simple as addressing your prospect with the word "Dear _____" can up your spam score. "Dear Friend" is the worst, but other combinations can also give you a strike. Another possibly surprising ding is the use of ALL CAPS. In addition to being electronically spammy, it translates to those big changes in tone and volume you'd expect from the ickiest of icky salespeople in real life.

They would probably also say something like, "Karl here..." as if secretly, they always wanted to be a news reporter. And if you think of it, a lot of Used Car Salesman do kinda sound like they're giving you the evening news. As a reminder, using your name as the opener is *no bueno.*

The Used Car Salesman is usually also keen to cut to the chase. Sometimes they will actually say those words or something similar like, "I'll get to the point..." or "Real quick..." In examples such as

Karl here, he just does it. I bet you need a CRM system! I have one of those! *Wham bam,* thank you Ma'am! Why go through all the niceties when you both know what you want, right? Wrong. You're just being gross, Karl.

Let's say you meet someone at a cookout and they mention they have a pickup truck. You're moving in a few months and thinking that having a new friend with a truck will be a bonus. You would never email them and say, "Dear Joe — Remember how we met at that party and you told me about your truck? Let's be friends!" Naturally, Joe is going to believe that you only want to be friends because he has a truck. And, he'd be right.

As a call to action, I don't hate the promise to give someone a call at a specific day and time. It just doesn't work here, except that now I know specifically when to turn off my phone and/or throw it into a pit of hot lava just to be absolutely sure I don't accidentally take Karl's call. The rest of Karl's closing line borders on Defeatist behavior which you may have noticed is a trend for The Used Car Salesman. Deep down, even Karl doesn't want to talk to Karl.

Advice for Resuscitation: Karl's opening paragraph has one redeeming factor which is that he referenced how we knew each other. This is what you want to do. You could even use something similar to the one (possibly two) decent lines in Karl's whole email, "If you recall, we met at the Coffin Convention back in March." After that, don't jump right into the thing they said about your product or solution. Again, remember your goal of making a genuine connection. What was it about them that was interesting as a person? What did you have in common? Was there anything you promised to share with them? Maybe an introduction to someone else, the name of a book, or a recipe for your favorite keto-friendly eggroll-in-a-bowl recipe? Here's a revised version of Karl's email for this scenario where you've met someone for the first time. You had a brief conversation, but not enough to warrant whipping out your phones on the spot to schedule a time to talk more:

> Hi Everett,
>
> If you recall we met at the Coffin Convention luncheon. In addition to our quick business connection, it was great to meet another keto person!
>
> As promised, here's that recipe we talked about for egg-roll-in-a-bowl. The key is the dash of rice wine vinegar. It makes such a difference.
>
> Would you be open to scheduling a call so we can continue our conversation? In particular, I'm interested in learning more about your services as a potential resource for my clients. Happy to share my world with you as well, and then we can mutually decide on next steps from there (if any). Maybe a keto-friendly lunch!
>
> Since you mentioned your schedule being a bit crazy, I'll give you a call on Friday at 2pm so we can coordinate in real time. If you have a calendar link or another preferred way of setting a meeting, please let me know.
>
> Looking forward to speaking with you!
>
> Sincerely,
> Karl

This requires that you make meaningful connections out in the real world, as well as online. In the same way you should be curious in your emails, be curious when you meet people in person. Even if you talk to someone very briefly before a conference session, aim to get one nugget of information that you can build on. Ideally, it's nothing to do with your business. At a recent conference where I was an attendee instead of a speaker, there were a few free minutes before the opening keynote. The woman sitting next to me noticed that I use a Surface Pro tablet and mentioned she was seriously thinking about getting one now to replace her MacBook Pro. After asking her a few questions, I learned that all four of her kids were finally in school full time, so she recently started her own business. I told her how much I love it, and offered to help her with some tips about how to get the best deal and maximize the features. We exchanged a few more cursory words *ala* "where are you from?" and "what do you do?" As the lights went down, I learned her name was Lucy, and we quickly exchanged cards. All in, we talked for about eight minutes. It's a similar scenario to what we've all probably experienced hundreds of times.

Here's why my approach to that conversation made it so much easier to email Lucy after the conference: Even though she asked me about me, I made it about her. I asked her questions and made sure that she did most of the talking. Here's a tip: When they are talking, you are winning.

When they are talking, you are winning.

As a natural Overwhelmer, this is something I've had to practice. It would have been easy for me to take 7 minutes and 30 seconds talking about why I bought the Surface Pro to begin with, how I use it in my business, and how I had the Surface Pro 4 then bought the Surface Pro 6 because my son just started high school. Oh, I actually have two kids, and *blah, blah, blah,* about me; because it's all about me. The lights would have gone done, and I'd have nothing but her business card — *if* I had managed, awkwardly, to ask for it.

Instead, my part of the conversation was mostly validating her, getting her to talk about the things she is the most energetic about, and offering to be of assistance.

This was a conference with about 3,000 attendees. No doubt Lucy exchanged business cards with dozens of other people. Most of those conversations were probably, "How's the conference going for you? Did you see that session on Feng Shui for Coffins?" followed by "Where are you from? What do you do?"

The eager beavers who follow up right away, possibly before the conference ends, will send Used Car Salesman emails. Others will send Egomaniac, Apologizer, or Overwhelmer emails that start with the dreaded and fatal, "I'm just following up...."

Since Lucy seemed keen on my offer to help with her Surface Pro adventure, there's no "just." It's easy for me to follow up, keep it simple, make it about her, and confidently ask to continue the nice conversation. In my example email above, I would simply replace the recipe context of my "As promised...." following up with something about the Surface Pro tablet.

Most importantly, Lucy is likely to remember me and be more receptive to my email over many others. She will remember our very brief conversation because I *listened* to her; I made her *feel* validated and interesting.

The truth is that most of the people Lucy met will wait too long to connect with her after the conference or won't follow up at all. They may even have Lucy's card on their desk at this moment collecting cobwebs. The reason they aren't taking action is because they don't know what to say. So, have something to say. Make sure it's something that they care about.

When you have something real to talk about, you don't have to resort to Used Car Salesman tactics. You don't have to say things that deep down you know might sound icky, but you do anyway because someone taught you that these are just things "real" salespeople say if they want to get the deal. Find and kill all of that.

When I was first learning how to read, I went through my mother's entire collection of the "Great Books of the Western World" to circle all the new words I learned. Mom wasn't exactly thrilled to see her gilded, leather-bound, copy of Gibbon's *The Decline and Fall of the Roman Empire* marked up in a five-year old's inky scrawl. Still, I think that exercise is one of the reasons I have always been an excellent reader. It's also probably why I have so much fun finding spam words in emails like this. If so inspired, feel free to do this for your own professional skill-building and potential enjoyment as well. How will you know if something is a spam word? As mentioned above, first identify any words that can be used to sell a cleaning product on television. Then, circle any other words that make you roll your eyes. Also kill any sentence that starts with any version of "Honestly…" While, despite popular belief, there's no concrete evidence that people who say things like "to be honest" are lying, it's hard to trust them in the context of all these other symptoms. Still, Karl was actually telling the truth when he said this email was going to be "truly unbelievable." I truly don't believe anything he says. #sorrynotsorry

6

RIP — The Defeatist

Cause of Death: Self-fulfilling prophecy of failure.

Primary Symptoms of The Defeatist:

- Painfully short emails
- Asking for a favor
- Frequent use of the word "please"
- Email upspeak
- Forecasting their utter defeat
- Anything that sounds like, "You or anyone you know. Literally anyone."

Defeatist Email Example 1

Subject: Just checking in

Hi Charlene,

Just checking in to see if you've thought about your Software Development needs for 2019? You're probably all set, but I thought I'd check in anyway.

If you or anyone you know need any upgrades, new projects or other implementations, perhaps you will keep us in mind?

My contact details are in my signature. Much appreciated.

Regards,
Belinda
<Phone #>

Coroner's Report: Defeatist emails are almost always painfully short. Yet, this is a good example of how someone can betray so much about their mindset and method, even when they are saying so little in the message. It feels like Belinda gave up hope before she even finished writing this email. She gets a rough start with the phrase, "Just checking in..." and then it just goes downhill from there. She barely gets to the second sentence before she's convinced herself that this thing isn't going anywhere. Starting with her statement, "You're probably all set, but I thought I'd check in anyway...." I can almost hear my mother's voice from the grave saying, "Don't worry about me. I'll be fine. Maybe I'll get fired and my landlord will throw me out on the street.... But, if you're all set, then you're all set. What's a girl to do?"

This is a good place to talk about upspeak. Upspeak is a rising inflection at the end of a sentence that usually indicates a question. However, a surprising number of salespeople suffer from abusing upspeak in statements. Since it's a vocal tick, it primarily shows up in live conversation, and especially in cold calls. For example, "Hi.... this is Mary (?) from Sassy Systems (?).... I'm calling for Charlene (?).

The way I break people of that habit is to make them say the words "question mark" every time their voice swings into a higher pitch at the end of a sentence. After a while, you start to hear it in your head without the verbal cue.

It should be easier in email. Yet, a lot of people use question marks inappropriately. Belinda's example is classic. It's so typical, that there will be many people reading this who won't see the problem with her question mark usage. Grammar rules aside, the problem is that it makes her sound insecure and whiny. As I used to tell my kids when they were little, "When you whine, you get nothing."

When you whine, you get nothing.

To some extent, The Defeatist sits at the opposite end of the spectrum of The Used Car Salesman. Where The Used Car Salesman is so confident about their sales ability they expect to win, The Defeatist expects to lose. I want to shake Belinda. (Come on, Girl! You can do this!) Actually, I want to shake her boss. It's rare for The Defeatist to be an entrepreneur or business owner. As mentioned earlier, sales emails can reveal a lot about larger issues in an organization. Sales messages can expose problems with leadership, culture, compensation, and structure.

This is a good example. Defeatists are usually made, not born. It would be worth further investigation to see if Belinda once had a good attitude which had been squashed over time. If so, my guess is that Belinda is using whatever time she didn't spend on this email on updating her resume. It's also possible that she's working under a compensation plan or sales structure that facilitates lackluster performance. One way or another, this is an open headcount waiting to happen.

Advice for Resuscitation: If you're Belinda's boss, there's more and different work to do than we are covering in this book. At a high level, just know that this email is a symptom of larger issues that must be addressed, such as the ones mentioned above. While I'm giving tips here to improve individual sales effectiveness, it's kinda like trying to outrun a bad diet. No matter how much we tighten up these emails, the day-to-day environment and infrastructure can easily sabotage that effort.

If you're a Belinda, give yourself a hug. It's going to be okay. You CAN do this. Read the advice that I gave to The Apologizer, starting with a hard look within. Depending on your environment, it might be tempting to blame your partner, your kids, your boss, your circumstances, or just plain ol' bad luck. Know that it is within your power to turn this around. More than that, it is 100% your responsibility to do so; nobody else. And really, why would you want to give that power to anyone else?

Some Defeatists are able to re-internalize their mission and deep sense of value. They just needed a reminder; a little boost. If that's true for you, consider this your personal pep talk. There's a reason you got into this business. What was it? What does it make you feel?

There are also Defeatists who look inside and feel... well, nothing. They simply no longer believe. Maybe they never fully believed in the first place. Or more likely, they wanted to believe (for themselves or others) so they squashed down that voice inside that told them this opportunity really wasn't a great fit.

Here's the thing: Life is way too short to do work that doesn't make you excited to get up on a Monday morning. There's a great quote by Howard Thurman that says, "Don't ask what the world needs. Ask what makes you come alive and go do it. Because what the world needs is more people who have come alive." This should not be confused with the advice I gave earlier about knowing *why* your clients and prospects need you. The 'why' is always more important than the 'what.'

The 'who' is also important. You should never resort to asking for "you or anyone you know" for two reasons: One is that you are attempting to build a relationship with a singular person. They should feel special. This statement gives you quota breath almost as bad as The Used Car Salesman. You wouldn't ask someone on a date and say, "Hey, would you or anyone you know like to go out for dinner with me?" If you did, they'd tell you to go with 'anyone' because they're not interested.

The other reason why the "anyone who" phrase is a death rattle, is that it exposes your lack of focus. Whenever I go to a networking event and someone says that a good referral for them is "anyone who..." I know they aren't hitting their revenue goals. In some cases, they probably aren't even making enough money for the business to survive.

The phrase "anyone who" is a death rattle because it exposes your lack of focus.

Focus is your friend. Clarity is power. Getting more specific about who you serve (and why) will bring you exponentially more money; not less. When you try to reach everyone, it's like yelling from the top of a mountain. Nobody can hear you, and eventually you lose your voice. It's painful. I've said it before and I'll say it again: Growing your business shouldn't be painful.

Take the time to identify who your bull's-eye target customer is on three dimensions:

1. **Demographic.** These are the qualifiers that could be on a pull-down menu, such as age, gender, role, industry, education level, and even whether they are married or have kids. If you have a B2B solution, the key here is to make sure your target is a person at a company, not a company. While it's a good idea to identify additional demographics for their company, it's in the context of where they sit in their role as a decision-maker. For example, you'd want to know their revenue goals and how many other people work there.

2. **Geographic.** Are they national, regional, or local? Getting specific about your geographic will not only help you focus your hunt, it will also help with time management. For example, you want to be well-organized and efficient if you are calling people in different time zones or trying to schedule coffee meetings across town.
3. **Psychographic.** Knowing that 95% of decisions are made in the subconscious, this is the most important place to find clarity and focus. It's also an area that has gotten more attention from marketers in recent years, particularly at the agency level. As a connector in your sales role, you have to get beyond the creative. In some of my sales training workshops, we walk through a detailed activity called *A Day in The Life of Your Ideal Bullseye Customer.* In this exercise, we outline their ideal prospect's day from the moment that person wakes up to the moment they are fast asleep. Sometimes we even talk about what they dream about and why they might wake up in the middle of the night. The most important aspects of this walk-through are thoughts and feelings. We land in their heads and hearts, and don't leave until we have explored every relevant inch.

Referring back to the Howard Thurman quote, this level of complete clarity about your ideal client isn't just about who is most likely to want to become your customer. It's more than who you can best serve. It's also about who you most want to have as a customer. As I always tell my kids about long-term relationships, "You have to be the right person *and* find the right person."

Remember: When you are in sales (whether you own the company or work for someone else), you are building relationships with *people.* That is your job. Let marketing worry about the billboards, the mountain tops, and the masses.

The Defeatist Email Example 2

Subject: A favor

Dear Charlene,

I've recently launched an executive peer group in this area, as you know.

I'm wondering if you would be willing to do me a favor and see if anyone else in your network might be a good fit? I'd really appreciate any referrals, as I only have a short amount of time to recruit at least eight members for my group.

I'm thinking it might even be worth you taking a look for yourself?

Either away, if anyone comes to mind, please let me know. If not, I understand.

Thanks,
Amelia

Coroner's Report: Here's the thing: I've met Amelia a few times, and we've had some decent conversations. She seems nice. Unfortunately, it sounds like she's now on a very short runway trying to launch a very big plane. There's a cliff at the end of that runway. It's not looking good.

Knowing this puts me in a very awkward position. Defeatist emails are always the most painful emails to receive because of the inner conflict it creates. Apparently, head trash is contagious. On the one hand, I do believe in the principle of being helpful and generous. I thrive on helping others be more successful. On the other hand, do I want to put anyone from my network of trust onto a plane that might run off a cliff?

I receive similar emails from others asking me for introductions into my network on a regular basis. Many of the senders are people I don't know as well as I know Amelia.

Let's put aside the many previously mentioned abrasions from which this email suffers. For example: all the "I" paragraphs, the email upspeak, and the "please let me know" weak call to action. The telltale symptom that puts this into The Defeatist category is the phrase, "do me a favor" in combination with a plea of desperation. Such Defeatist emails bring to mind images of ships sinking, trains going off tracks, and planes crashing off cliffs. It's Defeatist because they know they're going down, and they're grasping for any thread of hope. It's hard to watch.

Let's say I'm inclined to help. Perhaps I believe the plane will fly and/or that my desire to be helpful outweighs other reservations. Who would I refer to her? I have thousands of contacts on LinkedIn and meet dozens of new people each week through clients, networking, and speaking engagements. Even with the best of intentions, Amelia is making it too hard for me to help rescue her. The phrase "do me a favor" shows that she also believes this is a massive feat.

Advice for Resuscitation: It's important to build a solid referral network. However, the primary motivation for that initiative may come as a surprise to you. It's not so that you can get referrals. It should be so that you can build a community of people you trust enough to refer to other people you want to help. Giving is the number one goal. Receiving is a potential and positive side effect of that goal. That doesn't mean you never look to your network and client base for referrals. Absolutely, you should. A solid referral plan is an important part of any growth strategy. In fact, I strongly recommend finding and joining a referral network that is aligned with your type of business and core values.

Giving is the number one goal.

Unfortunately, too many business builders use referrals as a last resort or a weak, ancillary effort to other inbound and outbound strategies. That poor timing often adds an air of desperation which can sabotage the effort. Let's face it, the Titanic wouldn't have had much luck selling tickets after that whole iceberg thing.

The problem with The Defeatist is that they are thinking about getting referrals as an 'ask.' Done effectively, it's an invitation. It's offering someone the opportunity to position themselves as a connector, to help others in some valuable way, and/or fulfill a shared mission.

In this case, Amelia would have been well served to suggest a conversation about her group much earlier in our relationship. I'm guessing she didn't because she didn't want to "bother" me about it or seem like she was "selling." See also, The Apologizer. This tells me that she hasn't truly internalized the true power of a peer group like the one she is building. There's no question in my mind that this is the root cause of her struggle. If you don't believe in what you're building, it's pretty difficult to get others to believe.

Amelia should be thinking about why I would *want* to refer people in my network to her executive peer group. A meaningful conversation about my ideal target client and the mission of my business would have helped her make a very good case. Instead of it being a favor to her, she could have easily helped me see recommending her group as a favor to my business. More importantly, to my clients. Additionally, that discussion could have included some brainstorming about which connections she might be able to make for me in addition to my introductions through my network to her.

Anything positioned as a "favor" has the potential to strain a relationship, no matter how strong. Think carefully before asking someone to do something out of pure generosity or pity for a short-term goal. Whenever possible, create a win-win opportunity.

7

RIP — The Bridge Burner

Cause of Death: Ending the relationship before it started

Symptoms:

- Passive-aggressive language
- Playing hard to get
- Putting the burden of contact on the prospect
- Blaming the prospect for the seller's lack of process
- Anything that sounds like, "Apparently you don't want to be successful."

Bridge Burner Email Example 2A, 2B, 2C

First email (2A):

Hi Charlene,

I wanted to give you some value! Here are some articles that might provide insight for taking your business to the next level:

- *Article 1*
- *Article 2*
- *Article 3*
- *Article 4*

Best,
Chaz

Two weeks later at 8am (2B):

Hi Charlene,

Did you find my resources valuable?

Best,
Chaz

Later that day at 3pm (2C):

I'll take that as a no. Sorry to bother you. We will work on creating better content.

Chaz

Coroner's Report: Chaz may as well have jumped into a vat of marshmallow with that last message. It didn't have to be that way. Looking at the positive, his first email gets resuscitation points for brevity. If someone is going to give me homework, it's best to get right to the point. And, despite the whole "take your business to the next level" cliché, I appreciate the idea of leading with adding value. After that, it's a bit of a horror scene.

A seemingly "helpful" email with no call to action would seem to be an act of generosity. Except it's not. Your prospects will see through the thin veil of any free offer that isn't anchored in relevance. Chaz probably believes that giving free resources without any explicit expectation in return would make me think, "Gosh, that Chaz is such a thoughtful guy." Or perhaps he thought that if I read the articles, I would create my own call to action. I'd be so impressed, I'd be instinctively compelled to write him back and say, "Please Chaz! You must help me take my business to the next level!"

It reminds me of those guys who stand outside their store in the mall asking if you want a free hand cream sample. Then, if you so much as make eye contact, you find yourself somehow teleported into their store to be coerced into buying a $2,500 facial kit. After that, you develop radar for these things.

Then, Chaz waits two weeks to follow up again. Two weeks?! Chaz who?? This is a classic example of how the message betrays the method. Unfortunately, waiting too long between outreach attempts is a very common mistake among even very experienced professionals. When I first started working with one of my clients, their salespeople seemed to have a pretty good sales process. They used a solid CRM system that helped them keep track of calls and emails, tasks and opportunities. On the surface, the quantity of outreach seemed plentiful. The reps were even being (mostly) honest about their activity. So, why weren't they hitting their numbers? With so much outreach, why so little response? A lot of the initial email messaging wasn't bad. However, most of the reps were following a process like this:

Send an email. Set task to call in two weeks. Call and leave a message. Set task to email in two weeks. After that, it was a crapshoot whether they actually continued to follow up, or said they were following up with fake notes in the CRM, or abandoned the effort.

Relative to the message from Chaz, the two weeks between his first contact and the second is eternal. Like death. But then, it's as if he suddenly realized that he wasted two weeks of his life that he will never get back waiting for me to acknowledge his freely given wealth of knowledge. He asks me, "Did you like my free hand cream?" Then, mere hours later, he severs our connection. Typical Bridge Burner. Even though the last message is very brief and uses Apologizer language, Chaz isn't sorry. Chaz is a perfect example of how the shortest email can scream, "Please don't ever do business with me."

Advice for Resuscitation: Generosity is a key principle of sales as well as overall successful business. It's not a bad life strategy either. You should want to add value to others wherever and whenever possible. That said, check your ulterior motives. To be seen as a helpful and knowledgeable person is great. To share your help and knowledge with the exclusive expectation of receiving something in return, not great. Generosity is a principle, not a tactic.

> **Generosity is a key principle of sales as well as overall successful business.**

Always include a call to action. One of the hallmarks of The Bridge Burner is that they give up too easily. Timing mistakes aside, Chaz could have taken his generosity to another level with a compelling call to action that might have won him a conversation without seeming like he was just trying to fishhook me.

> Hi Charlene
>
> Your article on LinkedIn "Why Your Prospects are Ghosting You" was great! I shared a couple of your tips with my sales manager. In return, some of our articles might be relevant to you and your clients, based on the "Who" page of your website.

- *Article 1*
- *Article 2*

Would you be open to a brief conversation to discuss some of these topics in more detail? It would be interesting to get your perspective as a sales expert, and potentially inform some of our future resources.

What's the best method for booking time on your calendar?

Best,
Chaz

My revised version is a slightly longer first email, but the extra words pay off. It focuses more on "you" and "your" instead of "I" and "me." It adds value with depth. It has a compelling call to action that cares. It doesn't force or give up.

Overall, remember that your job is to *build* the bridge. This takes some diligence over time, a variety of tools, and dedicated effort. As one of my bosses once told me, "That's why they call it work. Otherwise they would call it playtime or leisure." Still, unless you follow a consistent process, it's going to feel a lot more like work than it needs to. What I typically prescribe is a multi-channel, multi-touch approach that works in lock-step with marketing. The timing is also important so that you have just enough breathing room to account for busy schedules, but not so much that you are starting over with each attempt. All of this is with the goal of getting the first meeting. Once you have that first conversation, staying connected is easy. That is, as long as you remember to book the next meeting. When prospects ghost you, it's your own damn fault for not setting the next day and time when you will talk again. If someone says, "Follow up with me in two weeks," then get something set on the calendar. I cannot stress this firmly enough; discipline around process will save your life.

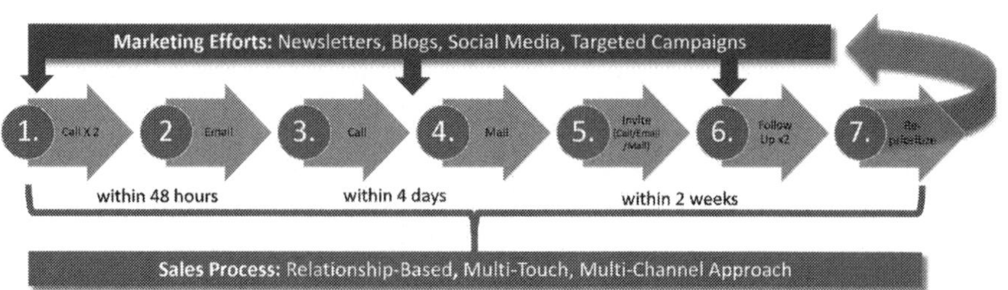

Bridge Burner Email Example 2

Subject: Are you looking for more gigs?

Hi Charlene,

By now, I've reached out at least three times with no response. I was wondering what kind of Speaking Gigs are you looking for?

The reason I am asking is, *<my event>* is taking place soon and I wanted to let you know about it just in case you are interested in more speaking opportunities. The people who participated in this event last year were able to speak at *<list of impressive companies and events.>*

Not sure if you are interested in getting these kind of gigs...

If you already have plenty of speaking gigs and not interested in growing your business at all, let me know and I will not contact you further.

No pressure,
Rosie

Bridge Burner Email Example 3

Subject: losing out on 10X results

Hi Charlene,

I've reached out several times since originally calling you, and you don't seem to be responding.

Yes, I actually wrote you all these messages personally. Not a bot, and I have the carpal tunnel to prove it.

I can only assume that you're not interested or you found someone else for <*these services.*>

Good luck,
Shia

Bridge Burner Email Example 4

Subject: hi, its me

Charlene

I'm just going to throw this out there. My feelings are starting to get hurt (LOL). I would have thought I would have gotten some sort of response from you. Please have the courtesy of giving me some sort of response so I can ensure I am not wasting your time nor mine.

Please click here to schedule time on our calendars.

Thanks,
Kanye

Coroner's Report: In terms of pure quantity, The Bridge Burners take up the most real estate in my inbox and the Email Cemetery. Rosie, Shia, and Kanye all suffer from similar problems. Like most Bridge Burners, they are Defeatists with a bad attitude. Where the Defeatist is probably thinking, "It's not you, it's me," The Bridge Burner is thinking, "It's not me, it's you."

Like Chaz, all of these charmers sent me a string of emails, each one worse than the one before. Somewhere along the line they thought, "Hey, let me sound like a jerk and see if that does the trick!" (LOL, amiright Kanye?!)

I'm sure nobody reading this is a jerk or wants to sound like a jerk. Sales is just work sometimes. Most of the time it does take several attempts before someone reaches out. The Bridge Burner allows that to get to them in a way that isn't helpful. It oozes out into their sales emails in little jabs. They think they are being subtle. However, statements like "unless you don't care about making money" or "do me the courtesy" are about as subtle as a two-year-old in a five-star restaurant after a full bag of Skittles. The two-year-old would probably be more welcome than this email.

Bridge Burners show a lot of warning signs. They tend to complain a lot. They will say things like, "No matter what I do, some prospects are just rude." They will be heard muttering words under their breath, such as "whatever" and "I hate people." Bridge Burners are also most likely to use popular non-verbal vocalizations such as the huffy puff, the grunty grrrr, and the exasperated sigh.

Advice for Resuscitation: If you suspect you may be a Bridge Burner or you have one working in your organization, it's an emergency situation. In addition to burning bridges which could have led to fruitful relationships, you're burning leads, effort, and time. Smell that? That's your revenue goal going up in flames.

Unfortunately, because Bridge Burners tend to place the blame on everyone else, they often don't get the help they need. This is where strong coaching comes in handy. An unbiased third party helps The Bridge Burner go from looking externally for their lack of traction to looking inward. Unlike some of the other personas who may benefit from a more gentle stream of meditative introspection, Bridge Burners need a fire extinguisher.

Another one of my favorite sayings is, "How you do anything is how you do everything." Chances are pretty good that if someone is at Bridge Burner stage, there are other areas in their life and work that would benefit from personal accountability. Where there's smoke, there's usually fire.

How you do anything is how you do everything.

Specific to the world of sales, the transformation needs to be from focusing on ending a relationship to focusing on starting a relationship. There's no such thing as, "What have I got to lose?" in sales. Even when you disqualify someone as a potential prospect, you don't know who they know. Your outreach attempt is a radiating point of connection. Potentially, everything you do has the power to extend beyond your immediate target or intention.

As a visual, write every email as if you have your arms open in ready embrace. Rework anything that might feel like you're crossing your arms or ready to hit the Unfriend button. If someone isn't responding to you, it's your responsibility to change your approach. No prospect owes you anything. It's not discourteous of them not to respond. You haven't even earned the right to expect a response. It's not them, it's you.

8

RIP — The Order Taker

Cause of Death: Creating a transactional relationship

Symptoms:

- Complete lack of emotion
- Sharing information without context
- Providing pricing before a conversation
- Weak or transactional call to action
- Including links to website menus
- Anything that sounds like, "Welcome to Burger King, may I take your order?"

Order Taker Example Email 1

Hi Charlene,

Thanks for your interest in our bookkeeping services.

Please click here for a menu of our services which range from simple invoicing and tracking expenses to full employee payroll and more.

If you have any questions, please let me know.

Best,
Mercy

Coroner's Report: Mercy's email is an all too typical response to an incoming lead. Any Order Taker reading this will be like, "They asked for more information, and I sent them more information. What's wrong with that?" Nothing is wrong with it if either A) you're selling a hot commodity in which "click here to buy" has proven to be successful, or B) you don't care whether they become a customer or not.

If B is true, then by all means, take that nice warm lead and shove it in the blast chiller. In this example, Mercy is setting herself up for a very long road through the land of, "I'm just following up..." If you've ever played the game Chutes & Ladders, this email is the equivalent of getting a lucky roll of the dice, only to hit the top of a red slide that sends you sliding down to a broken plate of cookies and a sore keister. In perfect conditions, you might get the customer engaged again. If you have enough time and the right ingredients, you can make more cookies. It's just a lot more work than it needs to be, and your chances of losing after that are greater than your chance of winning. Order Takers are on a slippery slope, my friends. A slippery slope indeed.

Next to salespeople who don't follow up on leads at all, The Order Taker is the quickest way to throw marketing money, time, and effort out the window. If we fired Mercy right now, she could easily be replaced by much cheaper software. Firing themselves isn't an option for Order Takers who own their own business.

Another way to think of Order Takers is as sales *ghosts*. They sort of look like they're doing something, but really it's like they're not there at all. There's no selling involved. This might be ideal for The Order Taker who has a lot of head trash about what it means to be in sales. They would rather avoid going down that rabbit hole. I mean, that's where The Used Car Salesmen and The Corny Cornballs live, right? Much safer just to sit at a desk and answer questions using the fine resources at hand. If that's not being a "salesperson," then maybe that's a good thing as far as they're concerned.

What's more toxic is The Order Taker who thinks they *are* selling. These are the people on your sales team who create havoc with everyone else in the organization. Order Takers will promise new clients yellow widgets, even though you only sell blue widgets. They will say, "But the customer asked for yellow, so we need yellow. Quick!" They don't know why the customer is asking for yellow, or whether or not blue would accomplish the same goal, or even if the customer is thinking about their goal in the right way. They just want to take the order. It's a travesty.

Mercy also demonstrates another common habit of Order Takers which I always find very odd. Even though I expressed interest via the internet, she linked me back to her website. Here I thought I was going up the ladder, and she pushed me back down the chute.

Meanwhile, she has no idea why I'm asking for information. She doesn't know whether I already have a bookkeeper and am considering a change, or I'm in desperate, painful need. She's not considering that I might be asking on behalf of a client, or several clients. Even though I clicked on a button that said, "Send me more information," Mercy is doing both me and herself a huge disservice by simply sending me information. She doesn't seem to care enough about me to find out why I need the information, make sure that what I'm asking for is what I need, or to position it in the right context.

Advice for Resuscitation: Incoming leads are precious! Keep them warm; don't make them colder. For goodness sake, if your prospect came from the worldwide web of too much information, don't direct them back there for more. Pick up the phone. If you get voicemail, leave a simple message and let them know you will also reply to their email. Use your email to get a conversation.

For example:

> Hi Charlene,
>
> Thanks for your interest in our bookkeeping services. Looking at your LinkedIn profile and website, there may be a few different ways that we are well-suited to serve you.
>
> To save you some time and ensure that you receive the most relevant information, let's start by scheduling a quick call to discuss your needs.
>
> Are you available next Tuesday after 2pm or Wednesday before noon? Or, if it's easier for you, you may use this link to find a mutually available time.
>
> Looking forward to speaking with you,
>
> Mercy

Don't listen to those Order Taker limiting beliefs that question, "Won't someone be annoyed if they ask for information, and I don't just send it to them?" Again, it depends on your goals. If you actually care about your customers and want to make sure you serve them in the best way possible, it's a good idea to let them know that. Confidence, curiosity, and connection are your friends. Your customers will always benefit from those things too.

Confidence, curiosity, and connection are your friends.

Will anyone get annoyed when you ask for a conversation to make sure you understand their needs before making their lives easier by sending the right information? Maybe. Do you want those people as customers? Probably not. These are the customers who beat you up on price, go out of scope, and generally torture you. If they won't let you act as their trusted advisor, let them go buy their yellow widgets someplace else.

If you still believe that some customers are genuinely too busy for a conversation, remind yourself (and them if necessary) that talking to you will save them time. You are here to make their lives easier. You care that they get the right information to inform the best decision for them. Ideally, you help them see that decision is you. Even if it's not, they are far more likely to remember and refer you.

Anytime sales are flat or suddenly flagging, it's worth investigating whether there's a whole lotta order taking going on. Sniff out your sales ghosts, even if it means looking in the mirror. Larger organizations may also need to consider a structural shift, including moving people around and possibly changing the compensation model.

Order Taker Example Email 2

Dear Charlene,

Per my voicemail, I am reaching out to you regarding your needs for office equipment.

Please find attached, a detailed brochure including specs and pricing for our extensive line of top brands.

Here are some highlights on a few of our most popular products:

> *<several paragraphs describing specific pieces of technology including pricing>*
>
> In addition to offering the best technology, we also provide the highest level of service. If there's anything you need, please let me know.
>
> Regards,
> Alex

Coroner's Report: There are some products that may seem to be inherently transactional, and office equipment is a good example. Yet, I have seen many emails very close to this one for a wide variety of products and services. If you can easily rework your typical sales email to be about office equipment, you're definitely an Order Taker. If you can read your email in the same monotone voice as a perpetually tired teenager in their first job at a fast food joint, that's a good sign, too.

One of the frequent complaints by stagnant companies and business builders is that they are sick of being treated like a vendor. Customers just want to know what, when, and how much. They want too much for too little. They got no respect.

You only have yourself to blame, Alex. Order Taker emails create this dynamic. It sucks, I know. Even in the best of times, it feels hollow. I can imagine Alex sitting in a stuffy room with a headset on, throwing a ball against his cubicle wall while his soul leaches out of his body. Alex probably drinks a lot. I mean, I would if I were Alex.

In the worst of times, being an Order Taker and creating an Order Taker sales culture can be financially devastating. You need relationships to differentiate yourself, form connections of mutual value, and build a sustainable business.

Let's say I happen to be in the market for a new printer. After spending too much time researching printers when I should be writing my book, I narrow it down to a couple of models. I spend more time reading reviews and comparing pricing through various sites. If by some miracle, Alex wins the spec and pricing comparison game, he might sell one printer. Neither one of us will know whether I bought the right printer. It will haunt me, while Alex will just go about his average life as an Order Taker. *Sigh.* Alex was in the best position to help me make that decision, and he didn't even try. Worse, as a growing business owner, I will probably need more stuff. Each time I'm going to waste too much time and angst. I may even spend too much money. Damn you, Alex! Why did you have to send me that stupid brochure when all I really needed was you! You're dead to me, Alex.

Advice for Resuscitation: If you are suffering from Order Taker-itis, your new goal is to shift both your thinking and your behavior from transactional to transformational. You must do this, even if the buyer seems to be asking for a transaction, i.e. "please send me the information and I'll let you know." It's for their own good, as well as yours.

In the buyer's mind, the transaction seems like the quickest and easiest path to getting what they want or need. The problem is that the buyer isn't an expert on your thing. *You* are the expert on your thing. Be their trusted advisor. Take a few minutes to discuss the real motivation behind why they are asking for your information. Dig into their layers of need, and be confident enough to make specific suggestions. In order to fully meet their needs, you must fully understand where they are today, where'd they like to be in the future, and what might be getting in the way of that transformation. Your job as an expert and trusted advisor is to help them see the impact of accomplishing that shift versus not changing anything.

When I attended CEO Group training through Vistage International, one of the instructors talked about measuring impact in four key areas of impact using the acronym HERD:

- *Hours:* While people know that "time is money," they often need your help to identify all of the places they are spending, saving, or wasting time. This could be time spent thinking and talking about their current situation, as well as time spent researching, executing, making mistakes, and starting over.

Measures of Impact

- **H**ours
- **E**motions
- **R**elationships
- **D**ollars

- *Emotions:* There are often a lot of negative emotions associated with the current state; they may worry about the future or be passionate about the potential of the future. Emotional impact is often missed because it feels fluffy to some people. Remember that people buy based on emotion, then justify with facts and logic. Digging into emotional impact is like printing money.
- *Relationships:* This is often closely related to emotion, and another place you may need to dig in a bit. Even if you're selling to a business, be willing to go beyond the work relationships. How is the current situation or setup helping or hindering the various interpersonal dynamics? How would solving it help? Even the most straightforward products can impact relationships. Just ask my husband and kids how much fun it is to be around me when the damn printer keeps jamming.
- *Dollars:* Connecting value to money should be the most obvious. No doubt, you've heard the term Return on Investment (ROI). Sometimes I also like to connect dollar impact to Return on Objective (ROO). The key is to expand your thinking, then educate your prospect on all of the places they could be saving, making, or wasting money. Perhaps it's worth getting a more expensive printer that doesn't need $35 replacement toner cartridges every flippin' month.

The transformation from Order Taker to a Trusted Advisor is one of the most exciting to watch. Not only does it feel better to the seller, it's a far more superior experience to the buyer. It allows you to build a relationship that both of you can trust. Furthermore, if you look through the HERD solution impact points, there's a case to be made that getting out of Order Taker mode checks all of those boxes for you in a big way, too.

Order Taker Example Email 3

Hi Charlene,

Our mutual contact, Alex, mentioned you were looking at various online advertising options. If you need prime ad space for a marketing push, we can definitely help. Currently, we have 50,000 unsold banner slots on The Graveyard's website for just $1,000, available on a first come first served basis.

This will be a great way to drive a significant amount of targeted traffic to your Charlene Ignites's site. Your banner campaign will run for 28-days on The Graveyard's widely read website, and the price includes the design of your advertisement.

Call me now to take up this discounted space or click here to check out the full specifics of the offer and get started.

Thanks,
Betsy Goss
Advertising Specialist

Coroner's Report: This is an example of a common mistake in believing that a referral is an easy ticket to Make-A-Sale Town. Instead of maximizing a mutual relationship to build a rich connection, Betsy goes right into Order Taker mode. It's a gamble. While starting with the mention of a mutual connection does stack the odds in your favor, going for the quick close is like rolling the dice so hard and fast that one of them rolls into Las Vegas traffic. Can you rescue it? Maybe. Is it a much riskier game than when you started? Definitely.

The rest of the email is very similar to Alex and other typical Order Taker messages. Most likely, all of these business builders and/or their company leadership believe that sales is a numbers game. While there is a correlation between activity and results, the traditional Dialing for Dollars thinking is flawed. That is, a formula that tells salespeople they must make 100 calls to get 10 meetings to get one deal. Believing in this formula requires willing acceptance that you are going to waste 90% of your time. Sometimes people will call it Dialing and Smiling in a vain attempt to breathe life into an otherwise soul-crushing practice. It's still a horrible strategy. If you translate that formula to email open and response rates, it's especially ridiculous. Yet, this is what Order Takers sign themselves up for: Just put it out there and see if someone bites.

One super clear way to know that this is happening is to see if you have any responses from prospects telling you that they're all set. Another sign is a lack of response altogether. Even clearer is the crushing two word reply, "Not interested."

Maybe they looked at the material you sent and maybe they didn't. Some email tools allow you to see what happened on their end. That knowledge isn't power when you're an Order Taker. You gave up your power by sending information without a shred of curiosity, caring, or connection.

Advice for Resuscitation: Respect the people in your network, and use their names with care. Referrals are a special gift. Don't you dare take that gift and throw it over the wall to the prospect like a UPS driver having an especially bad day.

Here's an example of an alternative to Betsy's email:

> Hi Charlene,
>
> Our mutual contact, Alex, mentioned that you might benefit from some online advertising. I'd welcome the opportunity to learn more about your business and your goals. It sounds like we may have more in common as well! Let's start with a phone call, then go from there.
>
> How does next Tuesday look for you?
>
> In addition to getting acquainted and any specific recommendations based on our discussion, my goal is to be a good resource for you on how to get the best results through online advertising overall. I know it can be a bit overwhelming!
>
> Talk to you soon,
>
> Betsy

Write your emails as if you care about building the relationship. Even better, actually care about the relationship. If you're not passionate about what you do to be a trusted advisor, you better find that passion or move to a new business.

Some final advice, if you're going to commit yourself to Dialing and Smiling, then for the love of all that's sacred, actually call people. You may want to change the name of the activity to Dialing and Drinking. You're gonna need it.

Post-Mortem

ALL OF THESE SENSELESS deaths have one thing in common: They are all making sales outreach unnecessarily difficult and painful for all involved. When you're forcing it, you're doing it wrong.

Whether you're reaching out to a warm lead or a complete stranger, take some pressure off both of you. Create a conversation. Be yourself. Take it one step at a time and keep moving forward through a series of mutually determined next steps. Own your value. Care.

Writing sales emails should be one of the easiest things you do. If you're struggling a great deal with your messaging, that means you have work to do on your mindset and methods. It may also mean you're confused about whether you're in sales or marketing. The messages that work best one-to-many are not the same messages that work well one-to-one.

How to Perform Sales CPR

As an easy summary on how to keep your sales communications out of the email cemetery, consider these CPR keywords:

C: Curiosity, Connection, Confidence

FOCUS ON: Being curious is the #1 most important characteristic of successful salespeople. Ask, don't tell. When your prospects are talking, you are winning. Keep the emails simple and put the real work into meaningful conversations. Aim for a genuine connection that builds trust and earns you the right to ask for the sale when the time comes. When someone asks for information or something out of scope, find out why and position carefully. Internalize the value of what you do, why you do it, and why others need you. When you truly believe, you're never bugging anyone.

P: People, Perceptiveness, Process

FOCUS ON: Sales is not a one-to-many effort. It's about being a person reaching out to another person. Remember that 95% of decision making happens in the subconscious. Therefore, you have to be an emotional detective. You also have to be willing to connect to your own programming and take out the head trash. Follow a consistent process with multiple touchpoints and a mix of methods. Once you get the first conversation, set the next one. No exceptions.

R: Relationships, Revenue, and being Real

FOCUS ON: Being in the business of trust. Your ability to build relationships will determine your success now and in the future through bigger deals, repeat business, and referrals. Taking your time to be more thoughtful will shorten the sales cycle. Being totally authentic and professionally persistent will make the relationship stronger. Revenue must be your goal, even if you are on a mission to help people. No money, no mission. You must be able to ask for the sale once you've earned the right to do so. Everything is better when you are more you.

PS: Pick up the damn phone.

How to Perform Sales CPR

Curiosity

Connection

Confidence

FOCUS ON:

Being curious is the #1 most important characteristic of successful salespeople. Ask, don't tell. When you truly believe in your value, you're never bugging anyone.

People

Perceptiveness

Process

FOCUS ON:

Sales is a 1:1 human effort. 95% of decision making happens in the subconscious. Be an emotional detective. Always set the next meeting.

Relationships

Revenue

Being Real

FOCUS ON:

Be in the business of trust. Relationships create bigger deals, repeat business, and more referrals. No money, no mission. Everything is better when you are more you.

Review Inquiry

Sharing is Caring

Hey there!

If you've found this book to be useful and fun, would you be open to helping others who are considering whether or not it's worth reading? Your feedback would also be hugely helpful to me, of course. (But you know, as a good steward of my own teachings, I try not to make it all about me.)

So, would you consider giving this book a rating with a brief review on Amazon or wherever you bought it? Online book stores are more likely to promote a book when they feel good about its content, and reader reviews are a great barometer for a book's quality.

If someone gave you a copy of this book, please leave a review on Amazon. Consider adding a picture of you holding the book as well. That increases the likelihood your review will be accepted so that others will see it!

Many thanks in advance,

Charlene

Know Someone Who Needs to Stay Out of the Email Cemetery?

Get this book for your staff, colleague, friend, or family member!

If you have found this book valuable and know others who would find it useful, consider buying them a copy as a gift. Special bulk discounts are available if you would like your whole team or organization to benefit from reading this.

Please contact charlene@charleneignites.com.

Would You Like Charlene "Ignites" DeCesare to Speak at Your Organization?

Book Charlene Now!

Charlene is a Professional Member of the National Speakers Association, and regularly speaks to groups of all sizes.

To learn how you can bring her message to your organization, email charlene@charleneignites.com or call 1-603-327-9064.

Bibliography

Federal Trade Commission. CAN-SPAM Act: A Compliance Guide for Business https://www.ftc.gov/tips-advice/business-center/guidance/can-spam-act-compliance-guide-business

Hoffman, Jeff (2019) 'The Ultimate Guide to Prospecting: How Many Touchpoints, When, and What Type' HubSpot https://blog.hubspot.com/sales/the-ultimate-guide-to-prospecting-how-many-touchpoints-when-and-what-type

InsightDemand. (2017) 'Neuroscience Confirms We Buy on Emotion & Justify With Logic & yet We Sell to MR. Rational & Ignore MR. Intuitive', Retrieved on February 20, 2018 from http://customerthink.com/neuroscience-confirms-we-buy-on-emotion-justify-with-logic-yet-we-sell-to-mr-rational-ignore-mr-intuitive/

Pradeep, A. K. (2010) 'The Buying Brain: Secrets for Selling to the Subconscious Mind' Wiley, Hoboken, NJ

Return Path Research (2017) "Mobile Is Now The Preferred Platform For Reading Email With More Than Half Of All Email Opens" https://returnpath.com/newsroom/mobile-now-preferred-platform-reading-email-half-email-opens

Shermer, M. (2011) 'The Believing Brain: From Ghosts and Gods to Politics and Conspiracies How We Construct Beliefs and Reinforce Them as Truths' Times Books, New York, NY

Schwartz, Barry (2009) 'The Paradox of Choice: Why More Is Less' HarperCollins, New York, NY

Thompson Walker, Karen (2012) "What fear can teach us' TEDGlobal on YouTube https://www.ted.com/talks/karen_thompson_walker_what_fear_can_teach_us?utm_campaign=tedspread&utm_medium=referral&utm_source=tedcomshare

Voss, C. (2017) 'Never Split the Difference: Negotiating As if Your Life Depended on It' HarperCollins, New York, NY

About the Author

CHARLENE "IGNITES" DECESARE has been a trusted advisor to leaders and organizations around the world for more 25 years. As CEO of Charlene Ignites, LLC and Founder of Firewalk Sales, she specializes in relationship-based sales. Her unique methodology is specifically designed for significant, fast, and sustainable growth that feels authentic and valuable to all involved. Before developing her personal brand into a full-time business venture, Charlene co-founded an innovative technology-enabled service provider called Tuition Advisory Services (now EdAssist, a Bright Horizons Solution at Work.) Prior to that, she spent 10 years at Gartner, Inc. where she created and grew a strategic sales initiative that led to millions of dollars in rapid revenue growth. Charlene has a B.S. in Communications from Emerson College and an M.B.A. in Sales & Marketing from Rivier University. She is a Professional Member of the National Speakers Association, a Nationally Certified Brain-Based Success Coach, and a Certified Sales Leader (CSL). Charlene lives in a beautiful lakeside home in New Hampshire with her husband, two children, and a black cat.

More about Charlene can be found on her website at **http://www.charleneignites.com** and on LinkedIn at **http://www.linkedin.com/in/charleneignites.**

Made in the USA
Columbia, SC
01 February 2022

55189566R00067